The Cello
and the
Nightingales

Patricia Cleveland-Peck is the bestselling author of twenty-four children's books, including *You Can't Take an Elephant on the Bus*, a radio play and a stage play inspired by Beatrice's story, and also writes travel pieces and non-fiction books. She came to know the Harrison family when living in a cottage on their estate at Smallfield, Surrey. It was while researching a biography of the four Harrison sisters that she discovered Beatrice's unpublished autobiography. She lives near East Grinstead, Surrey.

'Beatrice Harrison played while birds sang and she played while bombs fell during the Blitz. [An] indomitable musician with this blissful innocent spirit'

STEPHEN NACHMANOVITCH

T0273554

The Cello and the Nightingales

The Life *of* Beatrice Harrison

Edited by
Patricia Cleveland-Peck

Introduced by
Maria Popova

This Canons edition first published in Great Britain, the USA and Canada in 2024
by Canongate Books Ltd, 14 High Street, Edinburgh EH1 1TE

Distributed in the USA by Publishers Group West
and in Canada by Publishers Group Canada

canongate.co.uk

1

First published in Great Britain in 1985
by John Murray (Publishers) Ltd

British Library Cataloguing-in-Publication Data
A catalogue record for this book is available on
request from the British Library

ISBN 978 1 80530 018 2

Typeset in Bembo by Palimpsest Book Production Ltd,
Falkirk, Stirlingshire

Printed and bound by CPI Group (UK) Ltd, Croydon CR0 4YY

Contents

Illustrations

PHOTOGRAPHS

ILLUSTRATIONS IN THE TEXT

Introduction to Canongate edition

In the haunting interlude between two World Wars – decades before the Moon landing, years before the birth of television, a quarter century before digital music – a voice wild and free spilled its liquid rapture from the waves of a young medium, singing the history of the future, linking human consciousnesses around the world into a kind of planetary übermind. Here was an unprecedented collective experience rooted in our relationship to nature, which is also our relationship to each other.

The world's first nature broadcast of a wild creature in its habitat, and the first interspecies creative collaboration, the duet of the nightingale and the cello unspooling from the radio waves of the BBC from London to Melbourne to Mumbai was the dream of a young woman with an immense gift and an immense heart.

The second of what would be four daughters, Beatrice Harrison was born in the foothills of the Himalayas to a mother full of creative force and Celtic fire – Beatrice would remember her as 'someone apart from this world', endowed with 'quenchless vitality' – and an English mathematician father who had gone to India to teach engineering at a local school for miners, had fallen in love with the culture, had learned several Indian languages and had decided to stay. Having met Beatrice's mother at a music party on his first visit to England after eighteen years in India, he soon returned to the country he loved with the woman he loved and her grand piano, which would become her great solace as she found herself lonelier and lonelier on the other side of the world.

In the lonesome shadow of the Himalayas, Beatrice's mother sang and played daily – first to herself, then to her newborn infant curled up in her lap, and then to a new set of tiny hands and hammers and cortices forming in the womb facing the piano strings.

Music seemed encoded into Beatrice's being from the moment she was born. For all four sisters, music would be the great love of their lives; none of the sisters ever married. But in Beatrice, the gift was mixed with something else – some supravital energy, some uncommon spiritual fire.

When she was eighteen months old, her parents smuggled her into her first concert – the Band of the Royal Engineers, her father's regiment. As soon as she caught sight of a cello, she was spellbound. For weeks after the concert, she teetered around the house, proclaiming 'Baba play tello!' ('Baba' was her Indian name, the name her family would always use, the name in which she would sign her most personal letters, eventually compacting it to just 'Ba'.)

When the family returned to England – as much as her father loved India, he loved his wife more and couldn't bear to watch her spirit wither there – the wish was granted. One day, the door to the nursery opened and in walked her mother carrying something that sent Baba into 'a flying leap'. Gazing at the cello, she touched the strings and heard that same spellbinding tone her small body had already absorbed. What followed were days of 'sheer bliss', spilling into months, into years, never to remit for a lifetime.

Beatrice practised voraciously, proudly tallying the hours in her diary. The world was smaller then, and its music community smaller still, so word of her uncommon gift began spreading. At the age of nine, she was invited to perform for Pablo Casals – the greatest cellist of the time and, if one were to ask Yo-Yo Ma, the greatest cellist of all time – who encouraged her to unravel 'the eternal song' hidden in the cello. And so she did. At ten, she won the gold medal in a prestigious music competition with thousands of contestants of all ages. At eleven, she entered the Royal College of Music. When a wealthy widow with a love of music heard Beatrice play Beethoven, she sent her a bust that had once belonged to Jenny Lind — the greatest singer of the nineteenth century, known as 'the Swedish Nightingale', who had inspired Hans Christian Andersen's most beloved fairy tale.

It became clear to the girls' parents that by some blessed stroke of genetics and chance, they had produced creatures of uncommon talent, and their task was now to nurture its bloom into genius. Colonel Harrison left the army and devoted himself wholly to supporting his wife's devotion to their daughters, even though his own staunch parents considered music 'the work of the devil' and were, in Beatrice's recollection, 'terribly against it'. As much as he loved his parents, he loved his daughters more. The family moved where the best teachers were.

When Beatrice made her great London début at the age of twenty, the *Morning Post* declared her one of the world's 'most artistically satisfying violoncellists', exulting that 'music seems to be part of her and her realisation of the composer she interprets is so complete that her share as an intermediary is forgotten and the music becomes a living thing.' The *London Times*, taken with 'some undefinable quality in her playing', heralded her as exceeding even Casals. Everyone who loved her could see that music was her great love affair. Her sister remembers how often 'a faraway look' came over Beatrice in the middle of a party and she would suddenly vanish, the sound of her cello sighing moments later from behind the closed door.

Perhaps because her love of music felt so elemental, Beatrice came to see it as a basic human right, not an indulgence reserved for the elite. Although her family was far from royalty, she never lost sight of her many privileges, genetic and social. Still in their twenties, she and Margaret set out to bring the universal solace and rapture of music to people without access to it, playing cello sonatas to mill-workers and miners in a series of 'sixpenny concerts'. Those were the early days of broadcasting and recorded music, when the technology was both too primitive and too expensive to make the joy of music as ambient as air; the days before we made our Faustian deal with the technocrats who made music cheap and musicians poor so that we could stream it anytime, anywhere, with no recompense or thought of the souls from which the stream pours.

By the 1920s, Beatrice Harrison was celebrated as England's finest cellist. Composers were writing music for her, honoured to have her interpret their gift with hers. 'Please alter anything you like in the figures of my Concerto,' the venerated Frederick Delius told her. A family friend marvelled that she seemed to '*think* and *feel* in music'. And beneath all of this, holding all of this, was — in the words of another friend – 'the gentlest and kindest of human beings, without personal vanity and unfailingly considerate.'

And then she met the nightingale.

When the Harrisons' landlord suddenly needed his house back, they were forced to move. One afternoon, driving through the paradisal countryside of Surrey in the biting cold, they spotted a cottage for sale. It was entirely too small for the family, but in the setting sun it was radiant with a kind of spirit-warmth. Full of passionate intuition against all practicality, Beatrice's mother declared: 'This will be our home.'

Within a year, they built a music room where cows had once grazed and transformed the barren field around the cottage into a garden of blooming roses and delphiniums – a fitting tribute to the history of the place, rented by its first tenants in the thirteenth century for the annual fee of a bulb of gillyflower.

One dazzling spring evening, as bluebells and primroses bloomed in the woods around the house, Beatrice was overcome by the desire to play her cello in the fragrant open air of the moonlit night. She sat on a ramshackle bench under an ivy-covered tree and began with melodies she knew by heart, improvising on them as she went along. When she stopped, she suddenly heard the last note of the cello echoed by a voice in the trees. Trembling with delight, she began trilling up and down the instrument and listened in astonishment as the voice followed her in perfect thirds. She had never heard birdsong like that before. It came to her as 'a perfect miracle'.

Beatrice rose early the next day and ran to the local gardener to find out what that miraculous bird had been. Beaming with delight, the old man told her it was the nightingale, gone and now returned — beckoned, it seemed, by the cello. 'Don't ye let him go again.' She gave her word to keep the bird with nightly serenades. Every evening she wandered into the woods with her cello, playing and listening to 'the heavenly bird' – the migratory wonder that makes its voyage from sub-Saharan Africa each May, capable of singing more than a thousand different sounds composed into hundreds of complex musical phrases.

When the nightingale left to resume its migration at the end of June, Beatrice was already eager for its return. When the following spring painted the garden in bloom, her heavenly companion did return and they resumed their duets.

But as these nightly concerts went on to an audience of moths and rabbits, Beatrice felt the miracle was too great to keep to herself. She longed for others to share in it – people who, like her until that first spring in Surrey, had 'never heard the most exquisite bird sing'.

One morning after playing for the nightingale, she headed to London for a long-awaited performance, to be broadcast nation-wide. Radio was young then and television unimaginable. The BBC had been broadcasting for a couple of years, from the seventh floor of the old Marconi factory where the inventor of the radio-wave wireless telegraph system had first begun turning his invention into a commercial reality. 'The recording of sound and above all the broadcasting of it so that millions of people can enjoy it,' Beatrice reflected, 'has impressed me very deeply as one of the miracles of the modern age.'

Miracle collided with miracle in the laboratory of the mind, where ideas are constantly fusing with one another in the combinatorial wonder we call creativity: if all of humanity couldn't come to hear the nightingale, she realised, the radio could bring the nightingale to humanity.

No wild animal had ever before been broadcast from its natural habitat. The engineers thought it impossible. The bosses thought it a waste of time and money. After a 'hard tussle', Beatrice prevailed over the head of the BBC and persuaded him to send his producers to Surrey. Too nervous that all the commotion of cables and microphones would frighten the bird into silence, too nervous to fail in public, it has been suggested that the BBC hired an understudy – a professional whistler and bird imitator, in case the nightingale refused to sing.

On the morning of 19 May 1924, Beatrice Harrison watched 'all the paraphernalia of the BBC' spill into her garden for a live broadcast across the British Empire. About a hundred yards from where the nightingale sang with her each solitary night, they set up a sensitive microphone and hooked it up to an amplifier. Headphone cables and telephone landlines criss-crossed the sea of bluebells.

When night fell, Beatrice crept up with her cello, crooking her chair halfway into the most opportune ditch, knowing that 'the exquisite voice was there, under a thicket of oak leaves, ready to sing to his little wife.' For two hours, she played and played, hearing all kinds of curious noises – insects buzzing, rabbits nibbling on the wires, her donkey whinnying at the chaos of strangers – but the nightingale was nowhere in the symphony of night.

And then, suddenly, an hour before midnight, the world heard the exquisite voice singing to the cello.

Decades before fibre optic cable spanned the bottom of the ocean, the airborne voice of a spring songbird linked continents and cultures. People without radio sets phoned friends and asked them to press the receiver against their loudspeakers. The duet of the cello and the nightingale made its way around the world, reaching an estimated one million people – humans going wild for this improbable communion with another consciousness. Redeemed in her vision, Beatrice exulted in how 'the experiment touched a chord in their love of music, nature and loveliness.'

And so the experiment went on. The following week, the engineers returned. In London, journalists gasped at how her duet with the nightingale had 'swept the country', how 'a glamour of romance has flashed across the prosaic round of many a life'. A decade before Aldous Huxley observed that 'after silence, that which comes nearest to expressing the inexpressible is music', the director of the BBC, who had so doubted Beatrice's dream, boasted on the pages of the *Radio Times*:

> Milton has said that when the nightingale sang, silence was pleased. So in the song of the nightingale, we have broadcast something of the silence which all of us in this busy world unconsciously crave and urgently need.

That fateful summer of 1924 – the summer Beatrice Harrison became the first woman to play at Worcester Cathedral – people who heard the first broadcast journeyed to her garden by the hundreds, by the thousands, from China and Canada, Australia and America, China and Japan, arriving unannounced 'every hour of the day and night'. No matter how absorbed Beatrice was in her cello, she always broke away from the music room to show them the garden, moved by their enthusiasm for this fragile bird and its living reality.

Letters from around the world flooded in – more than 50,000, many addressed simply to 'The Lady of the Nightingales, England' or 'The Garden of the Nightingales, England'. Reading the outpouring of gratitude, Beatrice swelled with it herself – grateful to her mother, for having given her this gift; grateful to the broadcasters, for having taken a chance on her wild idea despite their scepticism; grateful most of all to the nightingale, for the honour of making music together – that triumph of consciousness, that unparalleled bridge between consciousnesses, that crucible of empathy.

An epoch before the world wide web was even the glimmer of a dream in a prophet's eye, Beatrice Harrison's improbable idea had sparked the first collective global experience around an event, in thought and in feeling, across space and time, via the world's first broadcast medium to bridge mind and matter. Radio – and its progeny in podcasting – cast its civilising spell not because it carried information – so had the telegraph – but because it carried emotion. It took a musician with a love of nature to remind us that we are creatures of feeling who feel most deeply with other creatures, and that in music we find our language of feeling, the native tongue of human nature.

When I first learned of Beatrice Harrison and the nightingales through musician Sam Lee's lovely contemporary recreation of her forest concerts, I immediately longed to know her, to know the spirit from which so uncommon a gesture toward beauty and wonder sprang. I found much written about her duets with the birds in the century since, but absent was her larger story and absent was her own voice. Through the rabbit hole of research, I eventually found my way to a used copy of *The Cello and the Nightingales*, published months after I was born and long out of print – Patricia Cleveland-Peck's lovingly compiled reliquary of Beatrice's diaries and fragments from the autobiography manuscript she never finished, entrusted in Patricia through her friendship with the two surviving Harrison sisters. Here was Beatrice, passionate and pure of heart, speaking to us directly. Here was a living record of loving the world through music.

It seemed a pity that so wonderful a story and a spirit would perish in obscurity. And so, believing that the best way to complain is to do something, I reached out to Jamie Byng of Canongate to see if we could breathe new life into this forgotten treasure, bringing Beatrice to another generation of music lovers and nature lovers, to all those who cherish what is most beautiful in the human spirit. After connecting Jamie and Patricia, chance seemed to smile upon our project – it turned out that they lived twenty minutes from each other in the English countryside. Swiftly a picture arrived of their smiling faces in Patricia's garden, and soon the book was being reborn. From its pages, Beatrice's voice rises clear and lovely as the nightingale's, free and sonorous with feeling as cello music improvised in a forest on a spring night.

Maria Popova

Editor's Preface

My husband and I lived in a cottage on the Harrisons' estate in Surrey for six years. Beatrice Harrison had died shortly before we moved there; but a close friendship with Margaret and Monica developed, and we heard many of the stories of their upbringing and their musical careers over the tea table. It was not until many years later, as a published author, that I suggested to Margaret Harrison that these stories should not be lost for ever, and told her of my desire to write a biography of the four sisters. During the amassing of material for this project Margaret presented me with the typescript of an autobiography which Beatrice had written towards the end of her life. Beatrice's voice came through very vividly and I read it with mounting enthusiasm. I realised at once that it had far too much verve and style simply to incorporate into my proposed book. I decided, therefore, to try to prepare it for publication. Meanwhile Margaret had found several other versions of the typescript, with additional handwritten material in notebooks. From these versions I have attempted to synthesise one coherent whole.

It would seem that Beatrice simply took an exercise-book and wrote down what she could remember of her life without reference to diaries or programmes. This has resulted in difficulties. Where events have obviously been described in the wrong sequence I have referred to diaries and other primary sources in rearranging her account chronologically. In several instances, for example, a series of tours has been compressed into one. Beatrice visited

Dresden in 1910 when she and May began touring in Europe but it could not have been until a later visit (they were there every winter for the next few years) that she met Tauber and heard his David, as he did not make his début which resulted in his five-year contract with Dresden Opera until 1913. Further examples occur in descriptions of American tours. Beatrice wrote this book towards the end of her life. While all the events she speaks of (with allowances for the 'exaggeration' she confesses at the outset) I take to have actually happened, it is not always clear exactly when.

I have restricted editing to correction of spelling and syntax, the thinning of Beatrice's frequent superlatives and adjectives of endearment, and the excision of some passages in which, always a dog-lover, she describes her pets in detail. To compensate, I have added letters and diary extracts (printed in a smaller typeface) which I felt would increase the reader's understanding of Beatrice's personality and friendships. I have tried to keep editorial comment (printed in italic typeface) to a minimum, so as not to interrupt the flow of the narrative too often. I have, finally, divided the memoir into chapters which I have entitled.

Editing this book has been an enormously interesting experience and one for which I am most grateful. My thanks first and foremost are due to Margaret Harrison, whose unstinting help and enthusiasm have made my task such a pleasure. I should also like to thank Mr George Cosham for practical aid in locating and retrieving valuable documentary items. My own family too deserve a mention for assistance in sorting out the rising tide of Harrison material which has threatened to engulf me. I am also most grateful to Lewis Foreman for very generous help and encouragement, and to Stephen Lloyd and Jerrold Northrop Moore for good advice. I should like to thank Bryan Crimp for compiling the Discography.

I should also like to thank all the authors, publishers and

copyright-holders of all material quoted: the Bax Estate for permission to quote letters from Arnold Bax; Lionel Carley and the Delius Trust for permission to quote Delius letters; the Trustees of the Sir Edward Elgar Will Trust for permission to quote Elgar material; Professor David Greer and Queen's University Belfast for permission to quote a letter from Sir Hamilton Harty; Gerald Moore and Hamish Hamilton Ltd for permission to quote an extract from Gerald Moore's book *Am I Too Loud?*; and the Society of Authors on behalf of the Shaw Estate for their permission to quote a letter from Bernard Shaw.

Patricia Cleveland-Peck

Introduction to the first edition

Between the wars, the name of Beatrice Harrison was familiar to most people in Britain, and to many throughout the English-speaking world. Not only was she the foremost British cellist, a friend and colleague of the leading conductors and composers of the time, but she was also known to millions because of her involvement in the first BBC outside broadcast of birdsong, when she played her cello in duet with a nightingale in her Surrey garden. The public went mad with enthusiasm about these broadcasts, and photographs, sketches and cartoons depicting Beatrice Harrison appeared in numerous newspapers and magazines. Now, twenty years after her death, her name has receded somewhat from public memory. For this reason I am delighted to be able to introduce her autobiography, for it is not just the story of a successful soloist but an account of an unusual upbringing, a fierce dedication to work, and an intense desire to bring music to ordinary people.

It is always fascinating to investigate the background from which a talented artist emerges. In Beatrice's case the background is rather unexpected. She was born on 9th December 1892 in the foothills of the Himalayas in India, the second daughter of a Colonel in the Royal Engineers who was at the time Principal of the College of Sappers and Miners at Roorkee. John Harrison was from a distinguished military family; his own father had been a Brigade Surgeon who fought at Corunna and Waterloo and he himself was a very fine soldier and leader of men in the Victorian tradition. He knew and loved India, spoke several Indian languages and had made profound studies of Indian customs and religions. He was loved and respected by the men he taught. Just prior to meeting Annie Martin who was to become his wife, he had spent fifteen years in India without home leave and he had no reason, at the time of this fateful meeting, to suppose that he would live or work anywhere else until retirement. Even as he fell in love with the attractive red-headed girl, his life began to change. For Annie Martin, although from an ostensibly solid middle-class family – her father was a civil engineer – brought into the marriage an element of Celtic fire and surprise which radically altered John Harrison's life and prospects. There was undoubtedly an unconventional and artistic side to her family. Her mother died young and Annie was brought up by aunts who had travelled unchaperoned to Italy in the early years of the nineteenth century; her elder brother Charles, a barrister, defended Janet Achurch in her divorce proceedings, after which he abandoned his successful bar career, married the actress, assumed the name of Charrington, and became an actor-manager living thereafter permanently on the brink of financial ruin; and Annie herself, unable to persuade her family to allow her to become a professional singer, nevertheless involved herself very fully in the musical life of the day.

It is significant that when young Mrs Harrison accompanied her husband to India, the one item she worried about was her grand piano. It became her joy and her solace and was of the greatest influence in the future upbringing of her daughters. India too played a part, for had Mrs Harrison not disliked the social scene so wholeheartedly she might not have spent so many long hours singing and playing the piano, first to herself and then to her infant daughter May (born on 23rd August 1890), and after-wards 'touching a chord in the yet unborn being' which was to become Beatrice. Very soon after Beatrice's birth the family returned to England. It is clear that John Harrison gave up a posting which he loved and for which he was extremely well suited, in a country which fascinated him, for the sake of his young wife who hated it. Such was his splendid character, however, that he settled easily enough into a War Office job before being given command of the Home Battalion of the Royal Engineers at Chatham Barracks. Fortunately he had a talent for getting on well with people and making a success of all he undertook, factors which applied no less when, a few years later, he gave up his career entirely in order to devote himself to the upbringing of his talented daughters. Monica was born on 3rd September 1897, and Margaret on 20th April 1899.

Mrs Harrison, her own singing career frustrated, had vowed that if she were to have musical children she would do everything in her power to help them. The environment was right, she was ready, and fate was to send her not one but four exceptionally musical children. May, the eldest, could at the age of three accompany her mother on the piano when she sang Schumann songs, she sang in tune before she could talk, and was blessed not only with perfect pitch but also with an exceptional musical memory. Beatrice, at the age of ten, won the Associated Board's Gold Medal out of four thousand competitors of all ages, when she had been learning the cello for only a year and a half. Both she and May entered the Royal College of Music at the age of eleven and won scholarships. It was on this account that Colonel Harrison retired completely from the army and settled in London, thereafter to assist his wife in bringing up his daughters.

It is difficult to imagine just how unusual a move this was in the days when the man was the undisputed head of the household and male dominance completely the norm. At one sweep the first hurdle at which many women artists used to fall was removed for the Harrison girls, that of having to make their art play a subservient role to the careers of the male members of the family. From the very beginning music was recognised as being of the highest priority.

In this atmosphere it is not quite so surprising that Margaret, the youngest daughter, could play Schumann's *Abendlied* on her violin before she was two years of age. Even before birth she had been engulfed in the singing of her mother and the music of her sisters for many hours of each day, and once born she found herself in an ambiance where scales, intervals and all the basic mechanics of music were as much the order of the day as those of speech itself. It would seem that Mrs Harrison had forestalled the import of any of the Japanese 'methods' with an infinitely more thorough system of her own.

From the material point of view life for the Harrison girls was comfortable, thus removing a second hurdle at which many would-be artists stumble. Fifty-one Cornwall Gardens was (and is) a substantial town house within convenient walking distance of the Royal College of Music. It had fourteen rooms including the breakfast-room, dining-room, school-room, guest-rooms, nursery, bedrooms, dressing-rooms, practice-rooms and a large drawing-room with painted walls which Mrs Harrison commis-sioned from a French artist. It is significant that when Margaret Harrison described the house to me recently she made no mention of the kitchen or domestic offices. From such things the girls were, for the time being at least, well protected. They were looked after by the usual number of servants for such an establishment, a cook, a tweeny and Florence the parlourmaid who came with them from Chatham. These were joined by Mark, the Tamil who came from their uncle's tea plantation in Ceylon; Miss Perry, the governess; Mrs Dunn, a piano teacher who came daily to super-vise piano studies; and Mademoiselle Amez-Droz, a violinist who came to oversee the violin practice. If Mrs Harrison did anything she believed in doing it well!

Every moment of the girls' day was meticulously planned. It is interesting to note that most of their diaries were kept during the mother's absence. If unable physically to direct events, at least Mrs Harrison expected to be shown a record of hours of work and progress made. The sisters rose early and the main part of the morning was taken up with violin, cello and piano. The main part of the afternoon was taken up with harmony and counterpoint. Lessons, going for walks, looking after their animals, afternoon rests on backboards, reading from the classics and playing games together were all fitted in around music. French and later German were fluently acquired from nurses or from living in the countries. It was thanks to Colonel Harrison as well as the governesses that the girls grew up with excellent general knowledge and culture for he had the gift of interesting them in many subjects. They enjoyed fun and diversions. Beatrice adored dancing and could easily have become a dancer. Margaret had a passion for animals which her mother allowed, realising that her daughter learnt thereby a valuable lesson in commitment. They all enjoyed theatre-going and May had rather a taste for parties and society. As attractive and talented young ladies May and Beatrice were much in demand to play in the salons of fashionable and titled hostesses. These were pretty occasions rather than those for serious music-making but the surprising outcome of one was the beginning of one of the greatest friendships of Beatrice's life. She and May had been asked by Lady Cynthia Crewe-Milne, herself a pupil at the Royal College of Music, to play at the home of her father Lord Crewe on the night that Queen Alexandra and King Edward VII were to dine. They brought with them their daughter Princess Victoria who adored music, and she and Beatrice became the closest of friends.

Princess Victoria, fourth child of King Edward VII and Queen Alexandra and favourite sister of King George V, has remained rather a shadowy figure. She and her siblings were described by their grandmother Queen Victoria, who disapproved of Queen Alexandra's liberal ideas on the upbringing of children, as 'wild as hawks', and she added, 'they are such ill-bred and ill-trained children I can't fancy them at all.' In fact they had a jolly childhood with very little emphasis on any formal education other than music. Lady Geraldine Somerset describes the three Princesses, Louise, Victoria and Maud, as 'rampaging little girls' and picks Victoria out as being 'very sharp, quick, merry and amusing'. But the girls grew up overshadowed by their mother's great beauty and in fact suffered from a lack of confidence which resulted in their being known as 'Their Royal Shynesses'.

Louise married the Duke of Fife and Maud became Queen of Norway, but Victoria was destined to remain the unmarried daughter and constant companion of her mother who, while loving her dearly, managed to curtail any personal life she might have desired. Queen Alexandra had no intention of allowing any German prince (of which the supply was plentiful) to marry her daughter, and Victoria was forbidden to think of marrying a commoner (although Louise had managed it), thus ruling out at least two men she was fond of. Victoria has been variously described as delicate, hypochondriacal, lethargic, childlike and embittered, but most have concurred that she was a very intelligent woman and must deeply have resented the restricted life at her mother's side.

Beatrice was in her teens and Princess Victoria in her late thirties when they first met. The friendship brought a measure of joy and interest into the Princess's life. She admired Beatrice's talent enormously and very much enjoyed watching her protégée succeed. She herself was extremely musical, playing the piano to a high amateur standard. She also loved occasional visits to concerts incognito, to hear Beatrice, and going down to Oxted to assist with the Harrisons' garden parties. Beatrice and she were drawn to each other, it would seem, by the very things which set them apart from other people. Princess Victoria by her special position in society was restricted from doing exactly as she liked, while Beatrice was similarly limited by her utter commitment to her art.

When the girls had progressed as far as they could at the Royal College of Music, Mrs Harrison looked around for suitable foreign teachers with whom they could study. Germany was still the mecca for musicians and it was decided that Beatrice should study there. Such was the closeness of the family unit that when Beatrice went to study with the eminent cellist and teacher Hugo Becker the whole family moved to Berlin where they took a flat and established a European base. May stayed with Beatrice until she left with her mother and Margaret for St Petersburg where she was to study with the great violin teacher Leopold Auer, while Colonel Harrison remained with Beatrice and Monica. Before she went to Russia, however, May 'shared' Beatrice's lessons in as much as she worked so closely with her that she benefited vicariously from Becker's words of wisdom. Later, when Mrs Harrison was in Italy with Beatrice, who was having some finishing lessons with Becker, she wrote May an incredible series of letters (one of which is quoted in this book) in which she attempted to impart to May the spirit of Becker's lessons to Beatrice. It is thus clear that throughout their childhood these girls never lacked the stability of a loving and supportive family background.

When eventually the studies were over and Beatrice was ready to embark on her professional career Mrs Harrison undertook all the arrangements for her complex tours and proved to be an astute and skilled businesswoman. In many ways she was in advance of her time for she showed a natural flair for publicity and spared no effort to promote her daughter, as is well illustrated by the famous 'nightingales' entertainments at Foyle Riding. All this, of course, so that Beatrice could concentrate on what was really important, music.

Concentrate she did; not only had she a great and undisputed talent but also a single-minded devotion to work. She was quite simply born to play the cello. She loved her family and her friends and she loved to laugh and enjoy herself, but even in the middle of many a delightful party at home, her sister Margaret remembers that a faraway look would come into her eyes and she would slip away from the company and a few minutes later the sound of her cello would issue from behind the closed doors of her room. The word 'practising' with all its dreary connotations was never part of Beatrice's vocabulary. Working with her cello was quite simply what she enjoyed doing best.

In many ways Beatrice never recovered from the death of her mother. Such loving and cushioning care was irreplaceable. Many great artists are a trifle impractical and absentminded, but in Beatrice's case any such tendency was compounded by the fact that she had been afforded no opportunities to practise independent life. Margaret, the youngest sister, took over as far as she was able and handled all domestic and financial affairs with a devotion (for she too was a violinist of the first order) which was quite exceptional. None of the sisters married, a fact not without precedent in the family for both Colonel and Mrs Harrison had brothers and sisters who enjoyed long, happy and useful lives without benefit of matrimony.

Mrs Harrison died quite suddenly in 1934. Although she was seventy-two years of age, somehow it seemed quite impossible that she should leave them. She had worn herself out with all the touring and planning and suffered a heart complaint. Princess Victoria, writing in sympathy when she died, said that Mrs Harrison reminded her of the chicken who hatches ducklings and wants to join them as they take to water . . . but that in Mrs Harrison's case, against all odds, she had done so. The image is telling for Mrs Harrison did much more for her daughters than could have been imagined or expected and she was sorely missed. At the time Colonel Harrison was also ill; he had suffered a fall and was bedridden, and although he lived on until 1936 in the next room, he was never told of his wife's death, so much was it feared by his daughters that the shock would kill him. Nevertheless, it is interesting to note that Beatrice ascribes his death to grief anyway.

Beatrice of course continued to perform and to tour but the death of Princess Victoria in 1936 and the advent of the Second World War were further blows to her. In the early '50s she gave concerts in London and Holland and her last appearance was at the Coventry Cathedral Festival of the Arts which was televised on 20th July 1958. This was a gala concert to raise money for the building of the new Cathedral, something which Beatrice cared deeply about. She played an aria by Marcello, *L'Amour de Moy* by Quilter and also accompanied Alicia Markova when she danced *The Dying Swan* to music by Saint-Saëns. After this she lived quietly with her sisters until she died in 1965.

May Harrison did make the break with her family and moved to London quite early in her career. She was a very fine violinist and had a distinguished career. Delius dedicated his Third Violin Sonata to her and she was a frequent visitor to Grez-sur-Loing. She recorded the First Violin Sonata of Delius with Arnold Bax, whose music she also admired deeply. As well as recording she also broadcast, played at the Promenade Concerts, and from 1935 to 1947 taught at the Royal College of Music. She died in 1958.

Monica Harrison was the least known of the sisters. After studies with Victor Beigel she made her début as a singer in 1924 when her voice was described as 'a light mezzo-soprano of agreeable quality'. A delicate, extremely intelligent girl who spoke French and German perfectly, Monica struggled all her life with poor health. Physically she was extremely slight having been born prematurely with defective tendons in arms and legs and this fact coupled with the nervous strain of performing prevented her from fully pursuing her ambitions. She lived quietly at home until she died in 1983.

Margaret Harrison was also a fine violinist. She made her début in 1918 and played as a soloist at the Henry Wood Promenade

Concerts in 1925. After Mrs Harrison's death, however, she rarely left Beatrice's side, accompanying her both physically and pianistically on tours and arranging programmes with violin and cello items in which they both played. It was during this period that Beatrice developed the passionate desire to bring the very best music to working people and she and Margaret played to miners and mill-workers in a series of popular 'sixpenny concerts'. Beatrice and Margaret had inherited from their father the great gift of being able to get on well with all types and classes of people and their complete lack of pretension endeared them to these mass audiences. Most people knew of Beatrice anyway because her nightingales broadcasts had caused such a sensation.

But interpretative artists eventually fade from public memory. If we ask ourselves how good a player Beatrice Harrison actually was, or how great her importance, the sources we must look to are the opinions of contemporary musicians and critics and the recordings she left behind her. Extracts from the cuttings books make for a monotonously rich diet of approbation, and I have avoided interspersing the text with the sort of laudatory comments that Beatrice herself would have found quite unnecessary. Here however, it may be of interest to note a few comments from critics at different landmarks in her career.

On her return to England after the very successful series of tours in which she and May played the Brahms Double Concerto some fifty-nine times, Beatrice made what was in effect her début in London at the age of twenty, with an orchestral concert. Here are the comments of the critic of the *Morning Post* on 3rd April 1913:

Such development of her natural powers has taken place as makes her at the present moment one of the most artistically satisfying violoncellists before the public. She expresses the real musical gift. Music seems to be part of her and her realisation of the composer she interprets is so complete that her share as an intermediary is forgotten and the music becomes a living thing . . . her tone is excellent in its roundness, her technique is very highly cultivated and her appreciation of the message of the music was of a degree of perfection and maturity proper to one of far greater weight of years. From every point of view her performance was brilliant.

On 17th June she played the Haydn Concerto in D, the Dvořák in B minor and Tchaikovsky's *Variations on a Rococo Theme*. The critic of *The Times* said:

Her playing was intensely enjoyable because of the presence of this undefinable quality in her playing, a peculiar clarity of tone and phrasing which can only be called eloquence.

After a recital at the Bechstein Hall where she played Richard Strauss's Sonata in F, with Hamilton Harty, the *Daily Telegraph* critic on 21st April 1913 said:

. . . it would appear that in London her position is established . . . in the past thirty years no violoncellist of her sex has approached her in all that goes to make the perfect player and artist . . . Nothing could have been more beautiful than her phrasing . . . it was the phrasing of a real artist. Moreover she has a pearly pure tone that is as even as possible throughout, even up in the highest thumb positions: an immaculate technique that is so sure that for her there exist no difficulties: while her right hand is simply magnificent. Not even Casals himself has a greater or easier command of a staccato, spiccato and legato bow or a purer style. It was in a word, violoncello playing of the very highest order: worthy to rank with that of a Casals or a Davidoff.

After recording the Elgar Cello Concerto, Beatrice was asked by Elgar to perform it with him many times. This work had received a disastrous first performance by Felix Salmond, due in the main to lack of rehearsal time, and Elgar acknowledged that it was thanks to Beatrice's performances that the Concerto grew and grew in popularity. Whenever Elgar himself conducted the Concerto he requested Beatrice as a soloist and she played it with him very often. As the critic of the *Glasgow Herald* said in 1921:

> But the great event of the evening was Miss Beatrice Harrison's perfect rendering of the new Elgar Cello Concerto. By her interpretation of this delightful work she has placed it amongst the truly great Concertos.

When in 1924 she gave the first public performance in England of Kodály's unaccompanied Sonata for Violoncello, another work with which she was to become closely associated, Ernest Newman wrote in *The Times*:

> Miss Beatrice Harrison has established the right to be regarded as the best of our British cellists, she enters with ease and ardour into the older formal music and the freer improvisatory style of the present day. She has made the Kodály Sonata her own. It seems to exploit every device of which the cello is capable and must be exceedingly difficult but Miss Harrison's mastery of it and of her instrument are so complete that the hearer is spared all sense of strain.

I have selected these comments as they relate to events which were of importance to Beatrice's career, not because they are the most lavish in their praise. (During one of the American tours, the *Boston Transcript* bore a banner headline, 'A Paragon! A Paragon! Miss Harrison transforms the violoncello concert into a stimulating event', and continues in eulogising vein for four columns.) They do, however, suffice to indicate what her contemporaries thought of her.

Every generation says about the last, 'Ah, but standards were lower in those days.' I have heard this said only recently about orchestral auditions that took place ten years ago. At the time when Beatrice Harrison grew up there was a piano in every parlour, and amateurs gathered together to sing and make music rather as people nowadays watch television, so undoubtedly there was much poor music to be heard. The greater interest in music, however, meant that in the upper echelons of the profession competition was just as fierce as it is today, and those who achieved artistic heights then were great musicians by any standards.

What has changed is public taste, and with it an appreciation of a different style of playing. We pride ourselves that we have 'cleaned up' technique and removed some of the excesses and flamboyance of the past. I think rather that string playing from another era rings strangely in our ears because of the change of style, in much the same way as the theatre voice has changed significantly. Henry Irving, indisputably a great actor, was thought of as 'naturalistic' in his day, but that is not how his recordings strike us now; and even the voices in the Ealing comedies are of quite a different calibre from those we are accustomed to hearing in modern films. One of the changes in instrumental playing has been in the use or misuse of rubato. Recently I heard someone comment rather disparagingly on Beatrice's rubato, to which Margaret replied dryly, 'Rubato is an art.'

Gerald Moore would seem to endorse this view when writing of Beatrice in his book *Am I Too Loud?*

Delius wrote his violoncello works with Beatrice Harrison in mind, and no wonder, for she had a poignant and luscious cantabile well suited to his music. Her playing of one heavenly phrase of the Cello Concerto lingers in my memory although it is thirty years since I heard the work. She sang on her instrument and had an infallible instinct for feeling where the muscle of the music slackened, where it tightened again, where it accumulated tension till the climax was reached. No woman cellist I have ever heard had, at once, a tone so powerful and sweet.

This we can discover for ourselves as fortunately by this time the science of recording sound was beginning to develop and Beatrice made quite a number of records (some of which are available for public listening at the National Sound Archive in London). Although nothing like the near-perfection of modern sound recording had been achieved at this date, nevertheless her early records are of very great importance. She recorded the Elgar Cello Concerto with Elgar by acoustic recording in 1919 and then re-recorded it with him in 1928 electrically. When we listen to these recordings, whatever our opinions about the quality of sound or changes of style, we are hearing the Concerto as Elgar heard and liked it. We are given a direct link with the composer, and for this all other exponents, whatever their interpretation, must thank Beatrice Harrison.

In many ways the most valuable contribution that Beatrice made to music was her involvement with the composers of the day. If fate was kind in placing Beatrice and her sisters in an environment so lovingly prepared for them by their parents, she was doubly kind in arranging that this should happen at the turn of the century, a wonderful period for British music. Beatrice inspired not one but several composers.

Her association with Delius is well documented, but Beatrice herself does not emphasise the implicit trust which Delius had in her. Having delivered his Double Concerto in 1916, Delius writes, 'please alter anything you like in the figures of my Concerto . . . I think it will sound well with orchestra.' At the same time he is thinking out the next work for her. 'I shall try to write you something for Cello and Orchestra but of course it will take time and the spirit must move me . . . but I will keep thinking of it.' The following month he writes to Beatrice in New York enclosing the addresses of some influential friends he hopes may assist her. 'Both these women,' he states, 'can be of use to you and will appreciate your genius.'

Not only Delius but also John Ireland, Cyril Scott, Herbert Hughes, Percy Grainger, Roger Quilter, York Bowen and George Henschel wrote for Beatrice. Arnold Bax was a close family friend and he too wrote for her. He understood her musical gift. He wrote to her in the '30s:

> Baba, dear,
>   I must just send you a line to thank you for the intense pleasure your beautiful playing gave me last night. It is astonishing that your first performance of this concerto should be so triumphant. I believe you think and feel in music, don't you?
>   Love from Arnold

This does not refer to the first performance of the Cello Concerto, which was given by Gaspar Cassadó on 15th March 1934, but to the first time Beatrice played it. She was in fact to give most of the performances of this work after the first. Bax wrote further to Beatrice:

My dear Beatrice

I want to write a line to thank you for your perfect playing on Tuesday. You are quite an inspiring person and I should really like to write more music for the cello, if you will play it . . .

and:

My dear Baba,

I want to tell you again how much I enjoyed your lovely playing the other morning. I cannot imagine a truer interpretation of what I meant writing the concerto . . .

and again on 1st July 1937:

My dear Baba,

. . . I may tell you, once and for all, that I think you are England's finest cellist and always have done and have said so.

Love to you and Margaret

Arnold

The enthusiasm of critics and the inspiration of composers mattered less to Beatrice than the enjoyment of ordinary people, watching her play being to many a moving aesthetic experience because of her great natural beauty ('Her poetic head always reminded me of a Botticelli painting,' said Cyril Scott) and the sweetness of her expression. She was in fact the gentlest and kindest of human beings, without personal vanity and unfailingly considerate. When, towards the end of her life, one of the young gardeners picked up the tea tray to bring it indoors for her and then stumbled and shattered the valuable tea service, Beatrice's only thoughts were for his injured feelings, and she convinced him that it really didn't matter!

In her autobiography Beatrice Harrison says: 'I stumbled many times in my endeavour to give pleasure to others.' I hope that her story will not only show her readers what a very faithful servant she was to her muse but that it will also give them real enjoyment, for such, she writes, 'has always been my ambition and my dream.'

Patricia Cleveland-Peck

1

'Baba play tello!'

I always think of my blessed mother as someone apart from this world. It was she who took us abroad and gave us the great chances which led to our lives in music. She was beautiful and young in spirit to the end of her days on earth. She had quenchless vitality and was of an ardent blend – Irish and Cornish. She had a passion for music and a deep understanding of it. Her voice was glorious and she studied at the Royal College of Music under Garcia and Henschel* but there was no thought of a girl from her background being allowed to become a professional singer. However, at the RCM she made many friends including two lovely Rumanian girls, Anna Maghieray and Alexandrine Ghika, and with them she founded a big choir in the East End of London which had tremendous success, the Princess of Wales, later Queen Alexandra, attending some of their concerts.

Her father Charles, a member of the Irish Martin family, married Sarah, a Cornish girl. He was nineteen and she was seventeen. Her family was one of great charm and temperament. I believe she and her sisters were amongst the first girls to travel to Italy

---

* Gustave García (1837–1925) had a successful career as an operatic baritone and taught for many years at the RAM, RCM and GSM. George Henschel (1850–1934; knighted in 1914), singer, conductor and composer, and first conductor of the Boston Symphony Orchestra, settled in England where he maintained his position as a singer of the first rank. He was professor of singing at the RCM, 1886–8.

unmarried and unchaperoned. They were all beautiful but most died before they were thirty.

My mother, her sister and her three brothers were brought up by two aunts. Her eldest brother Charles Charrington was a lawyer who later became a well known actor. He introduced Ibsen to English audiences. His wife, Janet Achurch, was the actress for whom Bernard Shaw wrote *Candida*.

My mother's sister Beatrice was very lovely, with the most beautiful golden hair. She never married and adored us children. She lived on the Isle of Wight where we spent all our holidays, always having a glorious time.

My mother really had to fight the Harrisons and the Lugards to make us musicians. Except for my beloved father they were all terribly against music and called it the work of the devil.

When my father came home from India, after a period of eighteen years without leave, he was invited to a great musical party to meet a young girl called Annie Martin. When he saw her copper-coloured hair and heavenly eyes and exquisite skin, it was love at first sight and this was increased when he heard her singing Schubert songs. He asked in a low voice to be introduced to her and lo, there was my future mother feeding the hostess's pet cat with blancmange from a teaspoon!

I understand from his sister, our Aunt Maimie, that my father tramped up and down his bedroom for a week, trying to make up his mind as to whether he dared to ask such a beautiful being to marry him and go with him to far-off India. After a time however, his mind was made up, and he did ask her. After a short courtship they were married and she sailed away on the old *Seraphis*, the last troopship to carry the wives of officers and men. As she gazed at her father's face while the thousand souls on board joined hands and sang *Auld Lang Syne*, she knew she would never see him again.

My father was a great mathematician. He had been head boy at Cheltenham and it was there that the other boys roasted him before the fire because he would not tell tales on a friend. He passed third into the Royal Military Academy, Woolwich where he was awarded the Sword of Exemplary Conduct. He served in the Afghan War and at the time of his marriage was Principal of a College of Sappers and Miners at Roorkee, in the foothills of the Himalayas. He came from a famous military family; his own father fought at Quatre Bras, Corunna and Waterloo. Like my father, he loved music and sang enchantingly to his guitar.

My grandfather was a great humanitarian. Having lived through and seen the horrors of battle at Waterloo, he made up his mind to become a doctor. This he did and when qualified he joined the Grenadier Guards as Brigade Surgeon. He married Sophia Lugard, aunt of the great Lord Lugard, Major R.J. Lugard DSO and many others. They had three children: my father, our Aunt Maimie and our Uncle Charles. Neither married and Uncle Charles followed in his father's footsteps, qualifying as a doctor and Brevet Colonel in the Grenadier Guards. He was the first Commandant of the Queen Alexandra Military Hospital at Millbank where he was known as 'the beloved physician'.

It seemed so strange that mother, from her romantic Celtic background, should marry into such an austere military family. Only my father was apart from the rest and their marriage was an ideal one. Father's nature was sublime, combining gentleness with born leadership. He had great patience but I think it was his sense of justice that made him loved not only by English people but also by Indians. The only one of his four daughters who inherited these qualities is his youngest daughter my beloved sister Margaret. She has them to the full and how often I have wished that I inherited at least one.

Exaggeration is one of my greatest faults, and although as a child I was called 'the willing horse' I am afraid that I stumbled many times in my endeavour to give pleasure to others, which has always been my ambition and my dream.

Although my dear parents were so happy, my mother always had a fear of India. The mysticism was so strange to her, the terror of the nights, the wild animals, the snakes, the heat and dust and above all the way of life. This she found limited, gossipy and boring. No, she could not bear it! She was very lonely although she was much in demand for concerts. She missed the stimulating cultured life she had so enjoyed with her friends in London.

It was therefore a great joy when May, my eldest sister, was born. The ayah was a very beautiful hill woman, quite young and very competent. She had a curious habit of blinking her eyes which May, a born mimic, imitated perfectly when only a few months old. This ayah did have a distressing side to her character as my poor mother found out. She herself had a young daughter who was growing more and more beautiful. The ayah was consumed with jealousy and one day drowned her own daughter in the well.

As the months dragged on, life for my mother grew sadder and sadder as she became increasingly ill. Her one joy was her music. In the evenings she would accompany father as he played his flute but as he often had to be away, many were the hours she spent singing and playing alone. Little May even as a baby showed a marked interest in music and would hum the songs of the Indian servants. As soon as she could reach the piano she began to pick out the airs herself. Mother delighted in playing to her by the hour.

I think all the music mother played and all her singing must have touched a chord in my yet unborn being which gave me an adoration for music.

When I appeared in the world however, my poor mother was so ill that her life was despaired of. Would either of us live? That was the question. The doctor, the only one on the station, was generally dead drunk and the nurse who attended her had a very violent and unpleasant temper. On top of that my father was called away on duty at that moment. The doctor did what he could and, under the influence of whisky, I arrived.

To commemorate my birth, unknown to mother some of the young officers took my sister May to the mess and each of them gave her a sip of whisky. Being only three years old, she was brought home terribly drunk, having thoroughly enjoyed herself.

Father was always rather anxious about me. As a tiny child I used to gaze through him and he questioned whether I was quite right in the head. This has been questioned often since!

From the earliest days mother said she knew her music had been instilled into me too. Apart from that, the only thing I have inherited from her is a head of curly hair which has been a great help to me throughout my career. However late for a concert, however tired on arrival, I had but to shake out my curls (I was known to the family as 'the woolly-headed noodle!') and all was well.

When I was a few months old we left India and after what must have been a terrible sea journey for my poor parents with two small children and an ayah who was hidden most of the time, we arrived in England. Most of the way May occupied herself in slapping me, with the idea of making me black, as she could not bear white children.

At the age of eighteen months I was taken to my first concert by my parents. The Band of the Royal Engineers, my father's regiment, was playing at the Queen's Hall. My mother was very thrilled and put on her best hat, the first time she had been able to wear it since her return from India. I also had my best bonnet put on my head and a blue sash tied round my waist. Off we started in a four-wheeler.

At the concert I sat between my dear ones, but I was so little that the seat tipped backwards and nothing was visible but the tip of a sun bonnet and a pair of white kid shoes. My mother righted me and it was at that moment I caught sight of the cello. I do not suppose that Sergeant Conker (how could I ever forget him?) was a great cellist but he and his cello certainly conquered my heart.

I was always called Baba, my old Indian name, by those I loved and for weeks after that concert, 'Baba play tello!' was all that mother heard. There was something about the beloved cello that drew me even then but I was not allowed to learn it at the age of two. At that time I was placed firmly on the piano stool and taught five-finger exercises and then allowed to dance. Mother believed that dancing was important in developing imagination and feeling rhythms and she used to bend my body back or forth and tie me up with a piece of string and leave me to roll up and down the floor! Nevertheless even then, there was a sort of discipline in our musical beginnings. Mother took the greatest pleasure and delight in teaching us and at the age of three May could accompany mother as she sang Schumann songs. As soon as we arrived in England May developed a passion for the street organs which could be heard so frequently then. She would rush home and pick out the tunes in the exact key, and thus it was discovered that she had perfect pitch.

Annie Harrison wrote of this to her friend Anna Maghieray who had returned to Rumania and in 1895 Anna replied, 'What talent your little girl must have for music, and from what you say she will perhaps some day be a great musician.'

About this time May was given her first half-size violin and thereafter this became her first love. We all continued our piano studies however, and throughout the rest of our lives each could accompany the other when necessary.

I remember at this time my parents sometimes gave lunch parties and May and I were allowed down for a few minutes at dessert. One day we were visited by General Sir Edward Lugard, a great soldier who had been through the Mutiny. He was my father's uncle and also my godfather. Whether it was on this account or because of his white beard, I imagined that he was in fact the Almighty, come down from heaven to visit us. He was very affable and I remember asking him if he were really God and if he had come especially today because we had meringues for dessert? I also told him a great secret: that we had had our hair washed that morning and that was why there were meringues for dessert. All this in a low tone in his ear. I can't imagine what he made of it! The real point was that mother always washed our hair in egg yolks to make it bright and on those occasions the whites were made into meringues – *et voilà!*

The old General always wore a wonderful ring, and what a fascination it had for me. Made of Indian gold it was very big and had a clear brilliant diamond in the shape of a heart in which I tried to see my face. My father told us the story of this stone. It was given by a rajah to my great-uncle for a service he had rendered him during the Mutiny (the General had in fact saved his life). The diamond came from the oldest diamond mine and the rajah told my uncle never to take it off, as wherever he went and whatever happened the ring would protect him. The rajah placed it on his finger and there it stayed until the day he died. Although his sister was killed and his wife died in a terrible accident, the old General was untouched and at his death, at a ripe age, the ring was given to his nephew to be given to me as his godchild.

Also at about this time a well-known portrait-painter came to paint a life-size portrait of my sister May with her violin. His name was Derwent-Harrison although he was no relation of our family. It is a beautiful painting and while the work was being carried out mother would take me to the sittings to watch. Sometimes the artist gave a party with dancing. Oh how heavenly that was! Derwent-Harrison was a great dancer himself and although over six feet tall he would ask me to dance the Washington Post. Three years old, I would grasp a finger of each of his hands and we were off. I would fling my legs up as high as possible so as to show my underskirt as I thought this was very pretty, being embroidered with forget-me-nots!

Not long after, my sister Monica was born and May and I went to visit a great friend of mother's. I longed to possess a baby to cuddle myself and as I gazed from the tea table my eyes caught a lovely cherub hanging on the wall. It was made of Italian olive wood and was very beautiful. While our hostess was talking to my sister I unhooked this ornament and took it in my arms and talked to it. Nobody seemed to notice I had stolen it and I took it home and showed my parents. They were very upset and told me to return it to our hostess. I wept bitterly, kissed my *bébé* and took it back. Mrs Fowler smiled and told me to keep it near me and to love it always. I still possess this Italian cherub and it hangs on the wall above my Indian shamah, always a great treasure, even if a bit of stolen goods!

When I was six years old we moved to Chatham, where my father took command of the Home Battalion. We had a heavenly, heavenly life there. All the young officers were enchanting and we children were thoroughly spoiled.

Father's adjutant used to come and tell us delightful fairy tales. They always ended with a faraway look and a sigh followed by 'and then they fell in love and lived happily ever after . . .' and we sighed with him in ecstasy. One day when he came in he was very distrait and forgot the important ending. 'Why can't they fall in love and live happily ever after?' I shouted. He looked very sad; it transpired that he had just asked for the hand of a beautiful girl with whom he was desperately in love, but been refused. How cruel we children were!

It was here, at 6 The Terrace, Chatham Barracks, that my sister Margaret was born, to the sound of the Reveille. She was a most beautiful baby with a sublime temper and a strong will. When she was old enough my mother went to register the birth. On the way she came across a woman stuffing a bun into her baby's mouth. The bun then dropped into the dust and the mother picked it up and without even wiping it, crammed it back into the child's mouth. The baby then began to choke in a most alarming manner. My mother looked aghast. 'You will kill your child,' she remonstrated. The woman looked at her and replied, 'Oh, what's it matter? It all fills.' Mother went on in a thoughtful mood.

She arrived rather breathless at the Registry Office and sat down in front of the clerk. 'When was the child born?' he asked. Mother could not think. Was it the 19th or the 20th of April? The image of the choking baby had taken all certainty from her mind. 'Then you had better go back and ask the mother,' said the clerk impatiently. Mother lapsed into hopeless laughter but felt she had better take a turn in the carriage and come back with the required information. All the way she kept muttering, '19th or 20th? 19th or 20th?' until she felt quite giddy. When she returned the clerk looked at her. 'Well, have you asked the mother?' 'Ye-es,' she faltered, not daring to admit she was the mother. 'And what does she say?' 'The 20th,' answered mother decisively, but to this day we are not certain, so like to give dear Margie a shadow present on the 19th and a real present on the 20th, just in case.

I had a great friend in those days, just one year older than I was. She was pretty and clever but always seemed to like me to do the things she did not dare to do herself. One Sunday she had a whole shilling in her purse and wagered that I would not dare to do two things. One was to hang onto my father's arm as he passed at the head of his troops and the other was to get the soldiers out of line. This seemed distinctly dangerous to me but I was never one to refuse a dare. The first thing was to get up to

27

the head of the troops where father was marching as only he could march, with his sword of honour by his side. I gulped and quickly caught hold of his arm, looking up at him. His eyes gazed only straight ahead. I could not keep up and he shook me off, so I skipped away, sixpence won! The next part needed more thought. Suddenly I had the inspiration to get between two of the soldiers and push them out of line. I gave the first a push and was turning to the second when the Sergeant-Major, his face crimson, lifted me high in the air and set me on the path. I felt dazed and shaken but found my confederate next to me. Her father, who had seen the whole incident and guessed who was behind it, turned to his little daughter with his staff plumes shaking with rage and hissed, 'Gracie, you goat!' He did not even look at me. Gracie cared not one jot but took my arm and we walked slowly to the Garrison Church where in the middle of a long and dull sermon she slipped me the shilling I had won. My own dear father never mentioned the incident to the day of his death!

1 Beatrice and her first cello, *circa* 1901

2 Margaret (Bébé) Harrison aged four

3 John and Annie Harrison on
their return from India

4 Two violinists, a cellist and a singer: Margaret, Beatrice, May and Monica in the nursery at Cornwall Gardens

5 Beatrice and May on the night they danced *Pavane* for
Fauré. May's dress was mauve, Beatrice's yellow

6 Beatrice in 1910, at the time of winning the Mendelssohn Prize

7 The Double Brahms: May and Beatrice at the time of the series
of tours on which they played the work fifty-nine times

8 Beatrice with her Pietro Guarneri cello made in 1739

9 Beatrice with
Eugen d'Albert
in Berlin, 1913

10 Delius and Beatrice in the
Harrisons' garden at The Waffrons,
near Thames Ditton. Delius
began to compose the Cello
Concerto there at Easter 1921

11 Beatrice rehearsing the Cello Concerto with Elgar
at Severn House in December 1919;

12 and recording the Adagio with the composer on 16th November 1920

2

'Mr Wood was very pleased'

My father always called May and myself 'the First Battalion' and Margaret and Monica 'the Second'. One day I was sitting in the nursery with the Second Battalion with my youngest sister, not quite two years old, sitting near me, her small angelic face utterly absorbed as she played Schumann's *Abendlied* on her exquisite eighth-size violin. I will never forget the picture she made when suddenly the door opened and mother appeared after a day's shopping in London. Ah, what was that instrument in her arms? I took a flying leap – it *was* a cello! The breath left my body, I felt rather queer. My dearest mother told me not to be an ass but to sit quietly while she undid the case. She had not wanted me to play the cello until I was big enough to hold such a large instrument and until then I had been learning the violin in order to prepare my fingers for the cello.

I gazed at the cello, I touched the strings; yes, it was the same tone that had penetrated my soul at eighteen months of age. The days that followed were sheer bliss to me, the only difficulty being how to hold the instrument as it was a full-size cello and I was very small for my age, so I could not possibly hold it properly. I would have the peg drawn out about an inch, put my knees together and lean the cello against them. It was much taller than I. Once a week I used to go to Rochester for lessons and the first piece I ever played was the Dream Music from *Hansel and*

Gretel. How I remember shutting my eyes while I played it and imagining the angels guarding the cello and me.

Mother with her musical daughters started the fashion in the Station for every little girl, whether gifted or not, to play the violin. This in some cases was rather devastating. However, it did give a wonderful opportunity to Signor Fasoli, the Italian music teacher whom my mother had discovered. From that moment he never looked back and his gratitude to mother was unbounded.

What fun too we had at concerts in Chatham. Mother encouraged our natural desire to share our music with others by performing before an audience. Our friend Sybil Thorndike, daughter of the Dean of Rochester, often participated in these events. She was a most gifted pianist and it was not until an arm injury spoiled her chances of becoming a concert pianist that she turned to the stage for a career.

The opportunity of performing with the RE Band from the earliest ages may have accounted for the maturity shown by the Harrison sisters when they first played with orchestras a little later on.

Whether in aid of the Waifs and Strays, The Soldiers and Sailors Fund or the NSPCC, these jolly concerts at Chatham attracted, as one contemporary newspaper put it, 'a large musical and enthusiastic audience including many of the élite of the town, the city, the port and the garrison and the surrounding districts.' Not only did May play the violin and Beatrice the cello but they also danced! 'Their accomplished dancing in costume,' continues the paper, 'and charming way of posing in the minuet as well as in the tambourine dance secured them a double encore. Their dresses were pretty and exceedingly appropriate . . . with music by their governess (piano) and Band-Sergeant Vicary RE (violin), the dances of these little people came as a delightful variation in the concert programme.'

Not long after it was arranged for me to compete in the Senior Division of the Associated Boards of the RCM and the RAM

Examination. This was a tremendous thrill and as long as I did not have to get to the top of the cello, nothing else mattered. The examiner* was a great adjudicator and I think he was rather amazed when I entered the room as the cello was still much taller than I. I grasped it and began a lovely Sonata of Marcello with all the feeling possible.

My mother had come into the room with me but the boy usher, mistaking her for my teacher, told her she could not stay. The examiner wore a skull cap which captivated my fancy to the full. He was very kind and all seemed to go well until the dreaded moment of sight-reading. I was hardly able to breathe as this was my weak spot. Suddenly the examiner rose and pushed my sister May, who was accompanying me, off the piano stool and sat down there himself. I was stumbling on as best I could when he turned and told me to follow his fingers and not to look at the music. He then played my part in the treble and his own in the bass which made it easy for me. When he rose his eyes were shining and he said, seeming quite elated, 'My child, some day I think the musical world will hear of you and your cello.' This was a great inspiration to me thereafter. I shall never forget the kindness of this man who so wanted a small cellist to pass the examination with distinction, which I did, that he helped her in her difficulties as much as he could.

Beatrice had passed the Association Board Examination in piano and violin at seven years of age. It is difficult to pinpoint the exact level she attained, for the original examinations were somewhat different from those held nowadays, aural tests for example not forming part of the syllabus until 1918. High standards, however, were required, and in some areas it is known that the examiners failed two candidates out of three. As Neville Osborne comments in a recent article: 'a glance at the early syllabuses

---

* Sir George Martin (1844–1916), appointed organist of St Paul's Cathedral on the retirement of his teacher, Sir John Stainer in 1888.

shows us a fearsome collection of scales in every conceivable combination.'
The Associated Board desired that their certificates 'should be regarded as
objects of distinction worthy of attainment.'

The examination which Beatrice took at the age of nine in the Senior
Division of the Associated Board, after only six months of study when
she was not yet tall enough to reach to the top of her cello, may have
been the old Preliminary Examination taken prior to Grade I, and the
Gold Medal which both she and May were to win at the age of ten was
then as now (winners receiving a book rather than a medal) awarded to
the candidate over Grade 6 who scored the highest mark in any instrument
or voice in the whole country.

Then came the time for us to move to London and leave the joys
of Chatham. Some of these pleasures I have never forgotten. The
dancing classes which Mother ran with the Admiral's wife, for
example. My sister May who was particularly strong was generally
detailed to dance with a little Scots boy who was a study in red;
red cheeks, red hair, red kilt and red knees, all of different shades,
whirling around to the strains of the polka! Then there were
the lovely Fancy Dress Balls given for the children. I particularly
remember one where May, who had such well shaped legs, was Sir
Charles Surface and I was Lady Teazle and as we were dancing we
looked behind to find our two small sisters, exquisitely dressed as
children in the period of Charles II, imitating our every movement.

My sister May had won a scholarship to the RCM and was
studying violin under Señor Arbós,* the great Spanish master. At
the age of ten she had established a record by winning the gold
medal of the Associated Board's Senior Department from three
thousand competitors of all ages and both sexes.

---

* Enrique Arbós (1863–1939), violinist, conductor and composer, pupil of Vieuxtemps
and Joachim (with whom he played the Bach Double Concerto), taught at the RCM,
1894–1915. He has been described as handsome, melancholy, alarming, and every inch
the Spanish grandee.

I continued with my cello studies and when I was nine years old I had the honour of playing for Casals. He was so sympathetic and gentle and when I had finished he told me always to make the supreme effort to attain '*le chant éternel*' on the cello: the eternal song which he himself attained so perfectly.

When we arrived in London I had been placed for tuition under Mr W.E. Whitehouse,* at the time cello professor at the RCM, as a private pupil, being as yet too young to attend the college as an Exhibitioner. Mr Whitehouse was the most lovable of masters. He very much wanted me to go in for the gold medal too, despite my youth. The day came and it seemed I had four thousand competitors. I had three separate examiners but by then I had mastered the sight-reading. Their faces never changed – they just nodded as I walked out. There was a whole month to wait for the result and one hundred and fifty marks to be won. At last the long envelope arrived. Dear father opened it – all was well, the cello had full marks for the first time, even if I had been the youngest.

A few months later I did enter the Royal College of Music, the Director, Sir Hubert Parry, making a special Exhibition for me known as the Director's Exhibition. It was a very happy time, all three of us were there. May was a brilliant pupil and my little sister Margaret, aged four, joined us, the youngest pupil ever to enter the RCM.** She studied with Rivarde,*** a brilliant pupil of Sarasate. She also studied harmony and counterpoint with Dr

---

* William Edward Whitehouse (1859–1935) studied under Walter Pettitt and Piatti. He was Professor of cello at both the RCM and RAM.

**At the time Beatrice was awarded the Director's Exhibition in 1904 she was eleven years of age, May was thirteen, and Margaret did indeed enter the RCM three months before her fifth birthday.

*** The New York born violinist Serge Achille Rivarde (1865–1940), after some years in the United States and in Paris, where he led the Lamoureux Orchestra, came to London and was on the staff of the RCM from 1899 to 1936.

Emily Daymond, a very dear friend. One day she said something to Margaret about 'a combination of sound'. Margaret, thinking she was referring to an item of underclothing then worn, put her finger to her lips and stopped her, whispering severely, 'Hush, we do not talk about them.'

I always loved the foreign element in the College with Arbós and Rivarde, and what fun we used to have at ensemble classes where we would read Schubert and Brahms Quartets by sight. I shall never forget the laughter caused by my left hand hopping about like a grasshopper on the cello strings but usually landing on the right note, nor the goodness of Ivor James, later cello professor at the RCM.

So the days went on and apart from our music we had to be educated.

French was almost the first language among the sisters, as was quite common at the time for children educated at home with French governesses and nurses. Colonel Harrison undertook their physical education, and regular exercise with dumb-bells, clubs and skipping ropes was taken. This was especially important for Monica who had been born prematurely and was very slight and delicate. She had a lovely voice, however, and at eighteen months could trill scales in perfect imitation of May on her violin. The sisters took daily walks and a daily rest on their backboards, during which their father read to them from Dickens and other classic authors.

When I was eleven years old I had the great joy of meeting Ellen Terry. The theatre had always been a great passion with father and he took us all very, very frequently – another great advantage in living in London. At that time my parents knew the critic Mr J. Comyns Carr and he and his wife took us one night to see *The Merry Wives of Windsor*. It was a never to be forgotten moment when I went round with Mr Comyns Carr and my sister to meet

Ellen Terry afterwards. She was so loving and so full of fun and fantasy. She asked me how old I was and when I told her she said, 'Ah, my dearest child, what would I not give to be eleven years old again', and she gave me such a kiss.

Then, lots of exciting things happened.

May, a brilliant child musician, made her début at an orchestral concert at the old St James's Hall with Sir Henry Wood conducting. She played a Bach concerto, the Mendelssohn Concerto, Bach's *Chaconne* and the *Introduction and Rondo Capriccioso* by Saint-Saëns. Her success was outstanding. Many famous musicians were there including Kreisler who subsequently became a close family friend. I was there to help present the bouquets, of which she had a great number, all heavenly, as well as a live Persian kitten in a flower-bedecked cage and a miniature Japanese tree in a tiny glasshouse. Feeling tired after presenting some of these, I sat for a moment in the front row, placing my own bouquet on the next seat. Lo and behold, a huge man very red and rubicund came and sat down heavily next to me . . . I suppose he was feeling tired too and there was nothing to be done about it. As May bowed with the air of a Grand Dame (she was thirteen) the said gentleman rose revealing my flattened flowers. When the family heard they just roared with laughter – so very, very heartless.

Shortly after this May went with Señor Arbós to make her European début in Madrid. She played with the Madrid Symphony Orchestra and gave many private concerts and recitals culminating in an invitation to play at the Palaces of the King of Spain and the Infanta. Everyone loved her and she was showered with presents including jewels from the Spanish Royal Family.

I was still at College of course. One day I played the Beethoven Sonata in D with a piano scholar. The next day I received a wonderful bust of Beethoven and a letter from the Hon. Mrs Eliot who wished me all success and happiness in my art and hoped that I would accept the bust which had belonged to the Swedish singer Jenny Lind.

Another thing I shall never forget were the heavenly dancing classes run by dear old Mrs Wordsworth.* How busily her eye roved round the feet of her pupils and those of the parents and chaperones. If ever dear father took us, he sat with his toes tucked under his chair and gazed straight ahead with a vague look!

Then unfortunately I became ill with rheumatic fever and had to spend a long time on my back. When I returned to College, being wheeled up in a long chair with my cello on top of me, I made a funny sight for passers-by. The Director himself used to welcome me at the entrance and I was allowed to take all my classes on the ground floor. Everyone was so kind.

Nevertheless the year was a very busy one for Beatrice. She always made a habit, as did her sisters, of noting down how many hours of practice she achieved each day. In 1907 she took this very seriously, adding in her diary totals for each week, each month and at the back of the book for the whole year, with much scratching out and re-adding of columns. The main conclusion to be reached is that arithmetic was not one of her strong subjects!

At the beginning of her diary for 1907 Beatrice wrote the following words:

On 29th May. I am making my début as a cellist at the Queen's Hall under the conductorship of Mr Henry J. Wood. I am playing the Saint-Saëns Concerto, the suite of Victor Herbert, the Boëllmann *Variations* and also Bach for encores. I *do hope* it will go well.

---

* Mrs Wordsworth taught the fashionable young how to dance as children and then prepared the débutantes for their presentation. Lady Cynthia Colville in her book *Crowded Life* wrote of her: 'loud voiced and rather terrifying but her kind heart and caustic wit shone through.'

Underneath is written: 'I will be very glad when my concert is over.'

Mother was always my greatest critic, not only for music but also for demeanour on the platform. Sometimes when I used to pass off my nervousness in extremely difficult passages with what I thought was a charming smile, she would give me a hopeless look. 'Why,' she said, 'do you look as though you've done up your mouth on either side with suspenders to give that idiotic look to an audience? Never do that again.' For this reason she installed large cheval mirrors in our practice rooms so that we could see and avoid any unpleasant expression. I have always been grateful for this for it is surprising how many musicians spoil their performance by unconscious grimacing.

At the beginning of 1907, however, Beatrice was more concerned with getting an adequate amount of work done. Her diary entries read:

> *14th January.* Began at 6.30 this morning and did 1¾ hours. After breakfast did almost another hour. Then a good hour's Ensemble. In the afternoon I did a good 1½ hours and 2 hours of lessons and ½ hour's piano. Arbos very pleased with the Brahms Quartet. Total 4½+ cello.
>
> *15th January.* Did 3 hours cello and good 4 English.
>
> *16th January.* Did nearly 5 hours of cello and 2 good hours lessons. ½ hour piano or very near. Composed a hymn.
>
> *17th January.* Began just after 6.30 and did good 1¼ hours. After breakfast did another hour and then 1½ hours Ensemble and ½ hour lessons.
>
> *18th January.* Went to Sir C. Stanford's Ensemble. He said I did too much vibrato. Not done much cello, only 3 hours. ½ hour piano and ½ hour lessons.

19th January. Done good 4½ and more of cello. Enjoyed
myself at Miss Barthums (party symphony concert and
German opera) but did not eat enough tea.
Total for week 28½ hours cello.

*The next week was an important one. The scholarship examinations at
the RCM took place in late January and early February.*

28th January. Did good 3½ hours or more. Played with
College orchestra Saint-Saëns Concerto. They were
pleased. Got sore finger. Did one good hour's lessons.
29th January. Got sore finger. Did 3 hours cello and 1½
lessons.
30th January. My first scholarship exam. Finger better.
Began the sight reading in the wrong key. Mr Bent
chuckled a lot. Over 5 hours cello.
31st January. Only 2½ hours Ensemble in morning. Played
to Hugo Becker. He was very pleased and so was Sir E.
Speyer and Lady Speyer. In evening played Brahms Eb
trio at College.
1st February. Not done much cello. Got up late and also
got cold. Done about 2½ hours cello and 1½ hours
lessons.
2nd February. Good 3 hours cello. In afternoon went to
Philharmonic Concert to hear Becker. He played
awfully well and the orchestra was too exquisite.
3rd February. Sunday. Did 4 hours cello.
Total only 18 hours cello for week.

*In spite of which Beatrice was able to write triumphantly 'Got it!' after
the final scholarship examination in February.*

*Beatrice here introduces some important names. This is presumably her
first meeting with Hugo Becker, who was to prove such an influence on*

her life and career. He was born in Strasbourg in 1863; his father was the violinist Jean Becker, known as the German Paganini. He studied with his father and also with Kündinger, de Swert and Piatti, and became solo cellist with the Frankfurt Opera and Professor at the Frankfurt Conservatoire. While Beatrice was studying with him he succeeded Hausmann as Professor at the Hochschule für Musik, Berlin. He was a very renowned teacher, and played in chamber ensembles with Schnabel, Flesch, Ysaÿe, Busoni, Marteau and Dohnányi.

Becker was by all accounts a severe, unbending and exacting figure. Henry Wood, in My Life of Music, *describes a piano rehearsal he conducted when Becker played the Brahms Double Concerto with Maurice Sons. 'Becker was a handsome Strasbourgian who knew the Brahms tradition probably as no one else in the world did. Sons thought he knew as much or even more . . . Becker pulled Sons up about every third bar, illustrating on his cello how he wanted him to play the violin part . . . by dint of exercising considerable tact I managed to prevent these two from coming to blows in my drawing-room.' Becker was known to have an intense dislike of the French cello tradition, stemming probably from his rivalry with Casals. He died in Munich in 1941.*

Sir Edward Speyer was one of the most generous musical patrons of the age. His house in Grosvenor Street was open to visiting musicians, and it was almost certainly here that Beatrice played to Becker. Speyer was a Privy Councillor and a banker of German origin. He was Chairman of the Queen's Hall Concert Board and he saved the Proms by forming a syndicate to ensure their future when Robert Newman, who had started the Promenade Concerts in 1895, went bankrupt. It is estimated that prior to 1915 he spent over £30,000 of his own money on British music. When anti-German feeling ran high during the First World War, Speyer's naturalisation was threatened with revocation, and, bitterly disillusioned, he and his family left for America.

The day after the scholarship examination the Harrison sisters went with their parents to Halberry, the house on the Isle of Wight belonging to their Aunt Beatrice where they spent many of their holidays. Aunt

Beatrice gave Beatrice five pounds, then a very goodly sum, for passing the scholarship exam. That week of the holidays Beatrice did twenty-four hours practice. By May she was back into her routine in London, her début looming ever nearer.

8th May. Good four hours cello. Went to Mr Wood to try the Herbert. He said 'Like all English artistes you are afraid to play too soft.' He did say that the execution was good.

9th May. Good 3 hours cello.

10th May. Good 5 hours cello. Felt very tired. A beautiful hot day.

11th May. Only 3½ hours cello. Went to Mr Wood's in the morning and Lady Marcus's* in the afternoon.

12th May. Sunday. Only 1½ hours. A string broke.

Nearer and nearer came the great day.

20th May. Good 6 hours cello.

21st May. Good 5½ hours cello. My concert dress is a white satin jibbah, quite plain.

22nd May. Good 4½ hours cello. Mr Wood was much more pleased with me.

23rd May. 3½ hours cello. Had last lesson with Mr Whitehouse before the concert. He was pleased.

24th May. Good 4½ hours. Had last lesson with Mr Wood prior to concert. He was pleased. Went to Madame Sheba and tried on my new jibbah.

25th May. Did good 6½ hours cello.

Total cello 36 hours for week.

---

* Lady Marcus Beresford, a well-known society hostess of the day.

Beatrice's first appearance as a cellist was successful. After one nerve-racking moment the concert went beautifully. Beatrice in her diary the next morning relates:

> Everything went off awfully well. Everybody was pleased. Had 20 bouquets. Mr Wood was very pleased. The *Times* critic said I was a musician through and through.

The full programme read as follows:

> Overture *Hansel and Gretel* – Humperdinck
> Concerto in A minor for Violoncello and Orchestra – Saint-Saëns
> Andante from Cassation No 1 in G – Mozart
> 'Dance of the Shepherdess' from Third Suite '*Der König*' – Halvorsen
> (first performance in England)
> New Suite for Violoncello and Orchestra – Victor Herbert
> (first performance in London)
> Rondo for Wind Instruments – Beethoven
> *Variations Symphoniques* for Violoncello and Orchestra – Boëllmann

After which it was back to normal, with College concerts.

> 5th June. Played at Magpie Society Concert,
> Old Loc. [Locatelli], Piatti and Whitehouse. I thought I played very badly.

Before the end of term, however, several exciting things happened.

Our great friend Lady Cynthia Crewe-Milne, who later became Lady Cynthia Colville, asked May and myself if we would like to play some trios with her on the night King Edward and Queen Alexandra were to dine with her father, Lord Crewe. She was studying at the RCM herself and played the piano most beautifully. We were thrilled.

As we entered the room we stopped dead – it was such a lovely sight. Queen Alexandra looked exquisite and the King most regal, but the one I gazed at most was their daughter Princess Victoria. She was so beautiful and gracious, but little did I dream that she would become one of our greatest and most beloved friends and that we would spend countless glorious Sundays at her home making music together. However, that evening when we arrived home mother asked us what had impressed us most. May said the Queen's beauty and I said the size of the King's leg! Mother laughed and asked why. I told her it was because I was so afraid his magnificent garter would burst.

When I was fourteen I left the College. It was a great wrench saying good-bye to Mr Whitehouse who had been so good to me but Señor Arbós, who although really May's professor, had become a great friend of the family, strongly advised me to go abroad to study. My beloved parents agreed but where to go? Paris under Casals or Germany under Becker? Arbos strongly advised Germany as Casals was so often away that his pupils saw little of him. Germany was at the time the musical centre of the world. May and I were thrilled, to study abroad was our dream of dreams.

Before leaving College however, I had the honour and joy of being chosen to play with Glazunov when he visited the College. I played his *Chant du Ménéstral* with him. That piece has always impressed me very deeply – it is so full of the utter sadness of life.

However, Beatrice's diary entry for that day concludes:

> Played the *Chant du Ménéstral* of Glazunov with Glazunov.
> He is such a dear old fatty . . .

How far from my thoughts that day was the fact that the next time I was to see Glazunov would be in his native St Petersburg where I would be playing as a visiting musician.

3

The Mendelssohn Prize

It was decided that I should study with Professor Becker who had a lovely house just outside Frankfurt. May was to come with me and we were to be housed at a girls' school, the Taunus Institut at Königstein.

How excited we were on the journey. We left Victoria Station at eight-thirty in the evening and boarded the ship at ten-thirty at Queensborough. It was a lovely unforgettable night and May and I stayed on deck for a while before going to bed. Somehow we knew that this was the first big step towards our future careers and we shivered with anticipation. The stewardess woke us at four-thirty in the morning however, feeling both tired and sea-sick. By five-thirty we had arrived at Flushing and felt better. Then it was across Holland and up the Rhine to arrive at Frankfurt at about tea time. We went round Frankfurt briefly in a cab before taking the train for Königstein. I was cross at having to leave my cello at the customs post at Goch. At last we reached Königstein at about nine o'clock, tired and travel-stained.

The first thing we asked for on arrival was a bath. There *was* a bath, we were shown it but it was full of beautiful pot plants and clearly had not been used for months! May was furious but I did not care, so thankful was I to tumble into bed. The next day the cello came up from Goch and we unpacked and had a restful morning. The girls at the school seemed nice and we tried to communicate in our almost non-existent German. In the afternoon we went to tea with the Beckers who were very kind and charming to us. I was to be allowed to study the great Dvořák Concerto. I had heard it once but once was enough. When I met Becker at Sir Edward Speyer's house he played it to us afterwards, and when he asked me which concerto I loved best I was able to reply quite truthfully – the Dvořák. How I loved it and still do, and how I was to work at it. It was a great effort for my left hand and blood from the fingers often covered the strings, but what did that matter!

The following day mother left for Berlin, which was to become the headquarters for the First Battalion for the next few years. We both missed her but felt rather grown-up to be left on our own. May still complained about the lack of bathing facilities and was presented with a pudding basin from which it took her hours to wash from top to toe. I only tried it once, but May persisted to the end. The other girls thought it incredibly funny.

On Saturday 15th August 1908 Beatrice had her first lesson with Hugo Becker. It went well although Beatrice was nervous. In the evening however the sisters were invited back to his house to play. According to May's diary she played the Bach Chaconne and Beatrice played a piece by Valentini and two Hamilton Harty works. There were twenty or thirty people present who were very kind to the sisters who thoroughly enjoyed the party and did not get to bed until the small hours.

They soon fell into the routine of the school and had lots of fun. They began to pick up German, having about an hour's lesson a day, and of course hearing it all round them. Walks through the beautiful countryside surrounding the school with the mountains in the background, were an unforgettable pleasure – as were the friendships they formed.

Often we went to concerts or to the opera. One of the girls, a beautiful Saxon girl with heavenly blue eyes, loved the cello. Once when we went to the opera together to see *The Ring*, or *The*

Mastersingers, she bought a little mug and gave it to me. I kept it but in the intervening period we lost touch with each other. Forty-two years later, I received a letter from a stranger who had been to one of my concerts saying that she was staying with a very sweet woman who asked if I were Beatrice, the English girl who had been working with Becker and was at school in Frankfurt. I too had never forgotten my dear Irma, for I knew it must be she and I wrote at once. I received an immediate reply from her.

17th May 1950
Dearest Baba,

Really during all these years passing by, was that name singing in my head. Tenderly and truly. And so you can believe how touched I am you remember me! Dvorak's Cello-Konzert and you! Both always seemed to be united in the same time and in enjoyable remembrance. I can hear it now, how long ago you played it first. Hear it in ears, mind, soul, heart.

My life here has much light and darkness. I lost my son (at the age of seventeen years) because he killed himself, afraid from political future and fearing the war . . . fourteen years are gone since he left us . . . my dear husband, who very often was ill, died also in 1944 and I am now living here alone in this little house and garden, working, reading, singing, playing piano . . .

Yours truly and ever
Irma

How lovely it is to know that there are some dear souls who never forget.

One day the whole school went on a tremendous excursion to Limburg and Ems, starting at seven-thirty in the morning and returning at midnight. How we sang and laughed. What fun too we made for ourselves in the evenings. Once we all dressed up, I was the fat cook, Fräulein Fischer, one of the teachers was a sweep, Irma was an Italian girl, Margaret, another pupil, was a Japanese girl, another teacher was a gipsy and May was the character Minna.

Another day the whole town was decorated for the Jubilee of the Grand Duchess of Nassau and we all went to watch the procession and see the illuminations and fireworks.

The Beckers were planning to move to Berlin and we were to follow them. Mother had already taken a small flat and we were to be joined by Father and the Second Battalion.

How lovely it was to be together again! We celebrated by going to Wertheim and having tea there; tea in tall glasses like beer and delicious German cakes. Then to the zoo, which delighted Margaret, nicknamed Bébé, whose lifelong passion for animals was already well established.

May's greatest delight was that she could take a proper bath again. She was always very keen on parties and in the evenings we went out a lot, either to make music or to dance. However this gay life could not go on for long. May had been accepted as a pupil of the great Professor Leopold Auer at St Petersburg and Bébé was to study with his colleague Nalbandrian, and the time came when they had to set off with mother. How brave she was to take them, for Russia was already in a state of revolt and it seemed quite an everyday occurrence for a young revolutionary to go into a café with a bomb in a fiddle case.* Indeed, Mother told us that once when the three of them were in a restaurant a bomb did go off near them, nearly wrecking the place.

But back to Berlin. The flat we had taken was an ugly little one, bare of furnishings. I remember the dining-room had electric

---

* After the failure of the Revolution of 1905, the revolutionary parties vigorously continued their activities in and outside Russia. The rising number of political prisoners in these years – from 85,000 in 1905 to 200,000 in 1909 – is an index of the intensified war being waged against them by the Tsar's security forces.

light but of such a very low wattage that it was difficult to read by. Father thought of a good plan; he placed a chair on top of the little square dining-room table, directly under the light, and mounted. There he could sit reading the paper without too much discomfort.

Mother had left us for three months. We felt lost! Father could read the German poets but could not speak everyday German. I spoke a little but without much conviction. Ida, our wonderful maid, never knew what to give us for lunch. Every day she would pop her head round the door and ask me in a loud voice, '*Was für Mittag?*' I, rather worried, would shout back the one word I was sure of, '*Heringe!*' This went on for some while. Father was so patient, but when Mother returned I noticed he told her in a gentle voice that he never wanted to see another herring.

Ida was tall and buxom with pince-nez spectacles on her nose and she wore a small cap which always fell forward when she spoke. She knew a great many folk-songs and Monica, my little sister who had such a lovely voice, used to enjoy singing them with her. It was touching to see them, one so tall and one so small, singing together with their whole hearts and souls united by the lovely old melodies.

Colonel Harrison had retired from the army in order to accompany and support his daughters in their endeavours and studies although he was only in his fifties. He wrote articles for the newspapers, especially on the subject of his beloved India.

Father, from his seat on the table, would gesticulate with his paper and tell us what had gone wrong with politics and India. We listened, looking up at him from below, sometimes joined by Ida who was most impressed although she didn't understand a word. We were rather a captive audience as we could not lay the table for supper until he descended!

My enthusiasm for my work grew and grew but one day I noticed a hole in the front of my frock from where I had leaned over the cello. Ida looked serious and patched it immediately but somehow that only made it more conspicuous. I only had one other frock for 'best' but with Mother and May away we went to far fewer parties as work took up most of the time.

And the cello was beginning to sing!

Nor was life dull. At this time Beatrice wrote in her diary:

6th January 1909. Had lesson with Professor Becker. He was more pleased with the Dvořák. He played the 2nd movement.

8th January. Went in motor taxey [sic] to the Kaiserhof with Mrs Kieborn and had *delicious* tea consisting of cakes and chocolate. After went to Wertheim as Mrs K. had ordered a shawl which never arrived. In the evening we went to the Becker–Marteau Quartet which was a simply splendid concert.

10th January. Went to my bowing lesson with little Renaud, my great professor hum ha! He is too killing and looks like a little old owl in his spectacles. Only 4 hours cello.

16th January. Professor Becker rather pleased (but not very) with the 2nd movement. In the evening Father and I went to the Singakademie to hear a pianist, a nice-looking young man but he did not play too well.

20th January. I went with Father and Fräulein Podlich [the sisters' governess known as Poddles] and Monica to try to get a suitable blouse for everyday. None to be got which seems extraordinary in such a large place. Walked home with Father. Felt very hungry.

21st January. Only 4½ hours cello. Went for a walk. It is

really shocking how old and lame the German horses
are. I am so thankful I am not a German horse.

22nd January. Good 5 hours cello. 1 hour French. In the
evening went with Miss Craig and Miss Coleman to
Rosenthal's piano recital. I do love to look at people at
a concert. There was one most peculiar person who
reminded one of Dan Leno.

23rd January. Good 5½ hours cello. 1 hour French. Ida
arrayed in her best departed to a grand ball. We went
for a walk and then I had a bowing lesson.

24th January Sunday. Ida came back from her ball at seven
o'clock this morning fearfully crimson and smelling
dreadfully of smoke, her petticoat far below her skirt
and her galoshes on. The poor thing had been two
hours on the way.

25th January. 4½ hours cello. 1 hour French. Went for a
walk. Heard that Mother is ill.

26th January. Went to my lesson. Professor Becker really
pleased with 2nd and 3rd movements of my Dvořák.
In the afternoon went to Tietz and got stuff for my
blouse and also a belt. After went to see illuminations
for Kaiser's fiftieth birthday. Crowds of people. I do
think German policemen are the *funniest* people.

By this time however, we were very worried about mother. The
news of her illness which I had noted in my diary was in fact very
serious as she had contracted cholera. It can be imagined how we
longed for her safe return. We had little news and time passed so
slowly but at last the day came, oh the joy was so intense for us!
Mother looked terribly ill but both my sisters were smartly attired
in red coats trimmed with astrakhan and long Russian leather boots.

We could not wait to hear all the news. Professor Auer had
thought so much of May's art as a violinist that when Kreisler

had to drop out of the great Mendelssohn Festival in Finland, he proposed that May should take his place. The great honour of playing at Helsingfors, however, almost did not take place. Mother had begun to develop cholera, at that time [early in 1909] rampant in Russia, and was lying in bed feeling desperately ill. The doctor (who happened to be Mussorgsky's brother-in-law) feared for her life but so great was her spirit and recuperative power that she was determined to get well and go to Finland. The night before they were to depart he left a sleeping draught for her and told May to give it to her with some hot milk. May put the milk on the little old stove but as it would not light she added more spirit and the lamp suddenly burst into flames which at once caught the curtains and before she could do anything the room was on fire. Poor dear May tried to put it out but went too close and her face and hair were badly burned. Mother leapt out of bed, dragging her blankets off the bed and using them to put out the fire. The doctor was called again and May's poor face was dressed with what looked like butter and flour. It was then tightly bandaged. The doctor told May not to take the bandages off until she arrived, so intense was the cold.

The next morning they started, Mother feeling terribly ill and May suffering intensely too. Little Margaret tried to nurse both of them. The doctor came to see them off and told them he had telegraphed the doctor in Helsingfors to meet them on arrival. After a nightmare journey of pain and discomfort they were duly met. The doctor took them straight to the hotel and was most kind and helpful. When he took off May's bandages however, her lovely skin was full of the most awful red weals. However, there was nothing to be done. Mother instilled some of her indomitable courage into May and sent her straight off to the rehearsal.

At the concert she played magnificently and her success was enormous. She played the Mendelssohn Concerto of course and as Mother and Margaret were sitting listening Margaret heard two

Frenchwomen in the row in front say that if May hadn't got such terrible skin, she would be quite pretty! Margaret needless to say could have slapped them but at the end of the concert her relief and enthusiasm were so great that she rushed right onto the platform and flung her arms round May instead.

After the concert Mother collapsed and it was some days before the three could resume their journey back to St Petersburg. After some hours they arrived at the frontier, there was a long delay and it was bitterly cold. At last it was rumoured that a bomb had been found on the train and a regiment of soldiers led by an officer, about three feet high and equally round, came to see if there were any foreigners on the train. They went from carriage to carriage and seeing the violin case on the rack and observing that Mother and May and Margaret *were* foreigners they proceeded to turn out all their bags. Everything from their two trunks was turned out into the snow. Night gowns, evening gowns, music . . . at last in the very bottom of one of the trunks they spied something wrapped in one of Margaret's small flannel petticoats. They poked at it and it went off – they fell back shouting incomprehensible commands at each other. Then a silence fell and they all looked at May who was laughing uncontrollably. She unwrapped the dangerous object and displayed . . . Margaret's new little alarm clock.

Listening to these stories, how thankful we felt to have our dear ones back with us again. Mother, however, nearly fainted when she saw the patch on my frock and little Monica with her stockings down to her knees. I had never been able to find any small enough for her in Berlin. Father was in his favourite shabby old suit and Mother looked at him and said, 'John, never wear that suit again, I will buy you a thousand . . .' This was always her threat and he was quite used to it, so he just smiled and kissed her, realising more clearly than we did how near we had been to not having her back at all.

★

After this my dear parents took a heavenly flat in the Kurfürstendamm. It was all decorated in silver and gold and was such fun compared with our previous poky and dark abode. The Kaiser and the Crown Prince passed every day on their way to Potsdam and there were lots of the processions that the Germans seem so to adore.

Margaret and Beatrice then joined the Königliche Akademische Hochschule für Musik in Berlin, and enjoyed themselves greatly. As usual Margaret, now aged ten, was the youngest pupil, a situation she was quite accustomed to by now. Beatrice wrote to her aunt in London with the news.

Kurfürstendamm 63
Berlin w. 6th October '09

Darling little Auntie,
 . . . I daresay you have heard that Baby and I are going to the Hochschule, or High School for Music, here. I am going because Becker is going to teach there for a year. I went in for my exam last Friday and Baby on Saturday. It is quite against the rules for anybody under sixteen to enter but they sometimes, very rarely, make exceptions for an extraordinary talent. In the summer Becker wrote to Professor Moser, one of the head professors there, to tell him of Baby's talent, so though she was far too young they allowed her to try, just to see how she really plays. The examiners laughed rather when she told them she was going to play Bach, but when she began their faces soon changed. She played Bach [Sonata in E minor] and after that the piano and was told to come on Monday to know the result. So on Monday she and I both went to see if we were accepted. It was the head man of the College who told us the result. He was very kind to me when I went in, and told me he was happy to say I was accepted. Then after all the cellists had been in, the violins came next. Never before

were there so many entries. Only seven out of the forty who went in were accepted. One by one the pupils came out, nein, nein, not accepted. People were amused by Baby and at last the fat old man who called out the names said 'Miss Arenson' (meaning Harrison) and Baby with rather trembling legs had to go in . . . in a few minutes she came out with a very red face. She had been accepted. Out of forty, almost all Germans and grown-ups, Baby had been accepted with the other six. It is so nice because she is so English and they have never had one so young . . .

Ever your loving niece,
Baba

I do not think anyone can dream what Christmas in Germany was in those days. Every house, however tiny, had its Christmas tree in the window and at the end of each street there was a big tree beautifully decorated. In the big stores every window illustrated a fairy tale; Snow White and the Seven Dwarves, Hansel and Gretel asleep outside the Witch's Hut guarded by the Angels. One vision I shall never forget was an illuminated crib with the Virgin Mary in deep blue and Joseph and the Wise Men by her side.

Near us there was a pet shop, filled with every sort of bird and beast. Whenever we lost Margaret we found her gazing into this shop window. She decided her first purchase would be a harmless snake, she loved snakes so. It cost one mark, in those days a shilling. Proudly she bore it home and thinking it might feel cold she popped it in May's bed while she arranged its permanent quarters. Alas, bed time came and she forgot to pop it out again. May slipped into bed with a sigh of contentment . . . what could that be wriggling so strangely? She threw back the bed clothes and there, looking at her with a friendly eye, was the shilling snake. To give sister May her due she did not shriek but simply tiptoed to Margaret's bed and gave her a little shake so that she could retrieve him and put him in *her* bed for the night. All was well and the snake lived for many years and his name was Ornstein. As time went on Margaret assembled a great collection of Macrolepis lizards, tiny tortoises, chameleons and fish. She spent every penny she possessed in that shop.

I must say I shared her love of animals and encouraged her to the full. My greatest joy was birds. We had about fifty canaries, many of which we bred ourselves. We had a room specially wired so that they could fly about. What I loved best was to hear the Master Canary teach his sons to sing. His cage was placed above covered cages containing about six young birds. He would sing to them and within about a month they would each develop glorious voices.

The British Ambassador in Berlin at that time was Sir Edward Goschen, an amateur violinist who became a life-long friend. He was very kind to the Harrisons who enjoyed his company. In fact May gave him violin lessons at one point which, if his letters to Beatrice were anything to go by, both enjoyed enormously.

... in fact you and May both spoil me dreadfully but I like it very much because I take such a deep interest in both of you which reminds me that I was so engrossed in my excellent lesson today (excellent as regards the lesson – only fair to medium as regards the pupil) that I forgot to give May the criticisms which I promised faithfully to return. I wish I could play with 'Keckheit', also that I was a 'Halbkind' – but such things are not for the agèd (accent on the ed please). You have no idea how patient May is with me: for an hour today she guided my trembling and gnarled hand up and down the fiddle, pressing the wrist at one moment, turning it up at another, jerking the elbow up, pulling it down, putting stray fingers right and trying (oh so hard) to guide the bow the way it should go! And yet the spiccato does not come! though I followed her instructions to the letter for at least an hour after she had gone. Once I thought I had got it but it is as elusive as the Scarlet Pimpernel . . . but May is really angelic, no one ever took so much trouble with me in the hey day of my youth . . .

Goschen encouraged Beatrice and May greatly and liked to attend their concerts whenever possible. Sometimes, sadly, his official duties conflicted:

I have my tickets and my musical secretary and I were going together. Now old Prince Christian of Schleswig-Holstein is staying with us until Wednesday and although I have tried and tried to make him go to the theatre that night, I have not succeeded. One of my secretaries who knows I would particularly like to go to your concerts was shaking with laughter at the futile efforts I was making to get rid of him that night. I still have some small hope that the Empress might ask him to dine . . . but I am afraid it is no go . . . why will you two always have concerts on Fridays which is the worst day of the week for me?

Many happy hours were spent at the Embassy making music. May and Beatrice were such friends with Sir Edward's son Gerald, known as Bunt, and his friend Tommy Lascelles that when the sisters toured Germany Bunt and Tommy followed them from town to town. Tommy Lascelles did ask Beatrice to marry him at this time but as throughout her life, it would seem Beatrice felt that however fond she might be of anyone, the cello came first and she gave so much of herself to it that there would never be enough left over to make anyone a proper wife.

In the spring I went to Tremezzo on the Lake of Como in Italy to continue my studies with Becker, who had a beautiful villa there.

Beatrice and her mother were joined for three weeks by another young friend, Cyril Scott, an extremely talented young composer who had also studied in Frankfurt. He also wanted to marry Beatrice at this time and although she did not accede, they remained friends throughout their lives and Cyril Scott wrote many lovely compositions for her. As well as Pierrot Amoureux, *written in 1912, he later composed* Philomel, Pastoral and Reel *and* The Melodist and the Nightingale *for Beatrice.*

We stayed at the Hotel Suisse, a delightful but dirty little inn in the next village. The room I shared with mother was tiny and bare but there was just enough room to flourish the bow. The scenery was magnificent.

Mrs Harrison wrote home to May:

> Fancy lovely white and red camellia trees on the mountains, it is so exquisite and the mimosa, such immense trees in full blossom, how you would love it, the sun, the mountains and the lake. The woods are full of flowers now, lilies of the valley will soon be out.

And how romantic it was to travel by gondola to my lessons. The Villa Balbianello had been built years before as a monastery and every sort of flower seemed to be growing around it in glorious profusion: roses, jasmine, freesias scented the air. The atmosphere was one of utter peace, of that world of which I dream so often, paradise.

Two other young cellists were staying there and studying with Becker and we met some English girls as well, so were a happy party.

In fact Beatrice, the only girl cellist, was very much the centre of attraction with her sweet nature and natural beauty. As her mother wrote home to May,

Baba went out with young Lais in the morning and in the afternoon with Renaud, they talk music all the time, they brought me some primroses gathered on the mountains this afternoon and Baba had a colour like a peach, she wears her old blouse and I am glad to say her hair looks long and curly and everyone thinks she is Italian.

Beatrice worked five and six hours a day and never lost sight of the purpose of the visit. As her mother continues:

The boys would like to take us on the lake by moonlight but the practical Baba says she would rather go to bed and get up early and work. She really is a spartan and beats me for I have rather a yearning to go about a bit but we really haven't the money for pleasure-making and Baba has come here to work and it is so beautiful that we must be content . . . Her hair is greatly admired although she will bunch it all up when she is practising, after I have curled it most beautifully, she doesn't care a bit about her personal appearance.

Beatrice's thoughts were with her cello and learning as much as possible from Becker. Mrs Harrison was anxious to impart something of this to May, so that she too could derive some benefit in her violin studies, as can be seen from this letter she wrote to May.

My darling May,

Baba had a marvellous lesson from Becker today and I find he works all his splendid variety of tone by working up and down from the fingerboard to the bridge, simply marvellous and a perfectly loose wrist. Baba finds it most difficult on the fingerboard but she is working very hard at it and is getting better by the day. Becker played a cres. climax today and explained exactly how he did it and the same with a dim. If you can't get a good tone on the fingerboard . . . experiment everywhere. Becker says that that is the secret, experiment for yourself and when you hear something you don't like, go on and on until you get what you want. He says that is how he still works. Always use your head and insist on your fingers and arm obeying you. The bow is the thing, he says you ought to be able to play with those two middle fingers in the way that your wrist is so loose. Never practise without your mind. He says some people practise very slowly or very fast but the inbetween times are the most difficult and he told Baba never to say I cannot get this tone or that, always I will. Today again he said always begin a cres. pp as there is hardly any limit to pp but unfortunately there is a limit to ff. I think Becker gets the effect of almost breathing as it were on a note, by putting his bow down on fingerboard and then working gradually towards bridge. It is just like a voice, try it and also in dim. passages the more quietness when the sound commences or when it ceases the better. It sort of leaves you with your mouth wide open and a sigh, it is wonderful. Baba is getting it in the cadenza of the [Rococo] Variations. You sort of open your vocal chords and let the sound gradually out, Becker treats his instrument exactly like a voice. Mind you sing your own passages. Baba's cantabile is excellent now but my very dearest May it wants so much patience . . . read Auer's rules and think about them. I am certain you will get wonderful climax if you begin as I suggest and don't stay on fingerboard and then try each note slightly louder than the last until the enormous ff is reached. Don't let any changement of position or finger weakness interfere with the one glorious and gradual cres. You have so great a gift that if you have the patience to work like that you must reach such heights, this is for your own great joy. Becker was telling Baba that she must use great discrimination in the way her A string is so light in comparison with the others that often in cres. passages it sounds louder and therefore she must let it go naturally. I wonder if I make myself clear in all this! And Becker says you must always play everything a little larger for a concert platform, you won't forget about that? Twice this morning Becker said 'Bravo' to Baba and he looked so delighted but he says Baba plays like a man but she must have all the tenderness and grace of a woman, what is a woman without tenderness and grace?

Don't trouble to answer this . . . I always feel I must give you a little sympathy and if possible, help.

Fondest love and many kisses from Baba and your ever loving Mother

Becker suddenly announced that he wanted me to go in for the Felix Mendelssohn Prize. It was a prize founded by Mendelssohn himself and anyone was eligible who had at one time studied at a German College. This of course did mean that there were a large number of entrants.

I could hardly believe it when the great moment arrived. We had to be at the Hochschule in Berlin at nine a.m. I had prayed to the good God the night before and in the morning I went off with my cello and dear Father's blessing. We were the first to arrive and gradually the waiting room filled up. The only friend I saw was the hall porter. Although I did not know him well he had evidently taken a fancy to the cello for he came up to me and said in German, with a big wink, 'I bet you, Fräulein, a pair of gloves that you'll win the prize.' I smiled wanly at him and went on waiting.

Suddenly the first name was called, then the second. The porter said that no one was allowed to leave the building in case a candidate failed to attend. At last I asked if I could have a room to work in and I was given one at once. Mother kindly kept watch and at last at five-thirty, I was called in. I began and as I played the heavenly music seemed to move the hearts of the Examiners for smiles wreathed their faces and they thanked me gently.

I went back to the waiting room and after a short while I was called back into the Examination Room again. The Chief Examiner shook my hand and said, with a beaming smile, 'You have won the Mendelssohn Prize.' I could hardly believe him and thanked him warmly but he interrupted my thanks, 'It is not me you should thank, but God who has given you this gift and your parents for the opportunity to use it.' I shall never forget those words, nor the truth of them. I reached home at seven p.m. amid the rejoicings of my family.

The next morning the correspondents of *The Times* and the *Morning Post* and the *Daily Telegraph* came to interview me. It appeared that at seventeen I was the youngest competitor ever to win, and the very first cellist.

I believe that when Sir Edward Goschen told the Kaiser about it, the Kaiser scoffed, 'An English girl, never. For golf perhaps, but music, no!'

Beatrice received many letters from friends, all delighted and proud that an English girl had won. A friend from the Hotel Suisse wrote:

I cannot tell you what it has meant to me to learn to know and love you all and to have a little share in this great thing you have done. It is an honour for England and the cello and above all for Becker. I believe you will have given him one of the greatest pleasures of his life . . .

We left our flat on the Kurfürstendamm and took two flats in one. It was such fun furnishing them and the cheque for £100 which I received as the prize enabled me to buy a lovely little suite of rococo furniture for the drawing-room. With the exception of one small chair which I have had for years in my music room, all was confiscated by the Germans at the beginning of the 1914 war.

After completing her studies with Auer in St Petersburg, May returned to Berlin to make her European début. She played at an orchestral concert in the Beethovensaal under Kunwald on 7th October 1909 (the Brahms and Glazunov concertos). On 21st October she played again in Berlin — Bruch's Scottish Fantasy and the Mendelssohn Concerto and Tartini's Devil's Trill Sonata. She was received with great enthusiasm.

For some while May and Beatrice had been preparing the seldom heard Double Concerto by Brahms, Opus 102. They played this in Berlin on 17th March 1910 in the Beethovensaal under Noë with enormous success and then Beatrice made her Berlin début with a recital at the Bechstein Hall playing the Beethoven G minor Sonata and the Valentini E major Sonata. In December 1910 she played at the Singakademie with Hugo Becker conducting. At last her months and months of work on the Dvořák Concerto were rewarded, Becker was satisfied, and the Berlin audiences were delighted.

4

Glorious Pietro and the Double Brahms

It was time for us to return to England. Father went a week before us, to 'prepare things' as he said. I always had the feeling, however, that the darling wanted to escape the journey home with us! He knew what it would be like with all the animals to transport. I must confess that our luggage was remarkable; besides the family, our dear maid Ida (who had exchanged her tiny cap for a sailor hat so large that she had to enter the carriage sideways), our old governess Fräulein Podlich and our Indian butler . . . we had at least fifty canaries, all the lizards and fish, the snakes, the tortoises, to say nothing of the cello, the fiddles, the music and all the hand luggage.

We were bundled into the train, the birds carefully placed on the tables by the windows, where they all began to sing. Next came the fish in tin cans from which I am afraid water spilled in all directions, then came the tiny South American tortoises and the lizards. The whistle was just sounding when there was a commotion – a nervous lizard from Mexico had escaped from his little basket. Ah, all was well, the porter had caught him and thrown him back through the window. All would have been well, that is to say, had he not landed in the hat of the French Attaché's wife, who had kindly come to see us off. What a scream! Why hadn't the poor little fellow landed in Mother's hat? She wouldn't have minded a bit, but the French Attaché's wife was so beautifully dressed. After much climbing and cajoling by Margaret the errant lizard was returned to his box and calm was restored. The birds sang, they looked so gay that quite a crowd gathered round our carriage door.

The crossing was perfect and at Euston there was dear Father's anxious face looking for us. Out got our large family and there was a big hired car waiting for us.

Soon we were back at our London home, 51 Cornwall Gardens. We all loved this house with its spacious drawing-room and our familiar nurseries and schoolroom. May and I had our practice rooms right at the top, up 105 stairs!

Mother had decided that as she was to be abroad so much with May and me, the Second Battalion should go to day school in Kensington. Both enjoyed this very much and both did very well in their examinations. They were in Father's care and his great joy was to read Shakespeare with them before going to see the plays. They went to the theatre very frequently as well of course as continuing their musical studies.

It was about this time that I met Mrs Almeric Paget, a very rich American woman who was unfortunately a semi-invalid. She heard me play and loved the cello so much that she made me promise to come and stay with her on her estate. I promised I would one day, but our immediate plans were to return to the continent. So much interest had been expressed in our playing of the Brahms Double Concerto that we had been offered a splendid tour. No one had heard this concerto played for many years and the idea of two young girls performing it seemed to strike at the imagination, so after a lovely season of concerts and parties at home May and I set off with Mother to Europe.

We first played at Dresden – what a glorious opera house and what delightful people. Schuch was the famous conductor of those days and Petri the first violinist. The night before the concert we went to the opera and as we knew one of the directors, we were taken round afterwards to meet Schuch and the singers. The opera was *The Mastersingers* and that is where we first met Richard Tauber who was singing the part of David. What a wonderful David he was. He was so charming to us that night and whenever we met him subsequently. He told us he was coming to hear us play the next night which he did, coming round to see us afterwards full of enthusiasm.

The next morning we had our rehearsal in the Opera House prior to the concert. After a rest we were having something to eat. It is a funny thing but Mother had always had a premonition that one day I would cut my thumb. I poo-poohed the idea as all our knives at home were terribly blunt. However, in the hotel room I was cutting a roll with a very sharp knife when suddenly it slipped and cut straight across my thumb. I will never forget the agony in Mother's voice as she asked, 'Cut your thumb?' I nodded, I could not speak. What to do? We were due on the platform in the Opera House in half an hour's time and I was not even dressed. Nothing would stop the flow of blood. The only thing was to get a doctor to sew it up, but no doctor lived near enough to do it in time. A message came from the Opera House, we were on in fifteen minutes. It suddenly occurred to the chambermaid who was full of sympathy to send for the Opera House doctor, who was always in attendance. He arrived, such a dear old man, with a leather case. He pulled out a needle, but had not brought any thread. The maid fetched a reel of ordinary cotton and with that the wound was sewn up. He then asked if I could touch the cello – I tried and the wound burst open again. More stitches were put in as I could not have a plaster. I still wonder how I put on my concert frock as the pain was beyond words, but I clenched my teeth and off we went.

The Opera House was full and the orchestra was waiting for us. We went straight on and as I began the great cadenza, I felt the strength coming back to me, although I must confess I felt very ill. I put my whole heart and concentration into the music and, staunching the blood during the 'tuttis', we managed to get through and end with a great flourish. The audience, who had had to be told as we started fifteen minutes late, gave me a fantastic ovation with shouts of 'British Grit'.

That night the swelling came right up my arm and the pain was terrible but I knew God was with me and I was able to continue my tour and not let my sister down.

When we returned to Berlin a few days later Sir Edward Goschen called on us to read one of the criticisms, which mentioned amongst other things that our ensemble was so perfect it was as if we had two hearts with but a single thought, two souls that struck a single chord . . . As he entered the room May and I had just finished a rather heated discussion about the interpretation of a certain passage in the Double Brahms when in triumph I threw my shoe at her and she broke her beautiful bow on my back. Sir Edward looked at us and smiling broadly read, 'two hearts with but a single thought, two souls that strike a single chord?' We all burst out laughing and I retrieved my shoe.

And so the tour continued and what a tour it was. One of the most amusing concerts was at Metz. The audience and orchestra were composed entirely of soldiers and the work was conducted as though we were on the march – not much possibility of making beautiful nuances! Nevertheless afterwards the General and his staff all congratulated us. My sister enjoyed having her hand kissed by a German general but when I was presented he thought he would like to kiss my cheek. I became very angry and immediately slapped his face. The staff looked shocked and I know that Mother feared that as a British officer's daughter I might at least be put in prison but no, he only jumped and did not seem to mind. It probably was not the first time!

We went on to Bremerhaven, the great port that was later to play such an important role in the war. The conductor's name was Flick and the orchestra was very fine. Before he began the Brahms,

Flick clicked his heels together, I suppose out of respect, and then flicked his baton all over the place, almost catching the head of my cello. More than once he sent me into helpless laughter and it was all I could do to keep on playing.

It was a great hop to Vienna. How well I remember the first time I ever saw that beloved city. It is impossible to describe the atmosphere left by all the great composers and musicians who have lived and died there and the real sense of the love of music which permeates this wonderful city – and the Viennese, what joy and love they gave us.

Our first concert was a very great one. I played the Dvořák Concerto with Nedbal, a close friend of Dvořák. He taught me a great deal for which I have always been grateful. In the interval outside the artistes' room, a quartet of cellos began to play. We opened the door and there, seated outside, were the first Cellist, Hugo Kreisler (brother of Fritz) and three others playing Kreisler's *Liebesfreud*. It was such a charming tribute and touched us deeply.

We travelled all over Austria, always meeting with courtesy and enthusiasm for the cello, which is what I longed for. The tour comprised many garrison towns, where the officers would appear in gala uniforms – white with all their medals and their wives in full evening dress – a great tribute to two young English girls. The platform was always filled with heavenly flowers of every variety.

I shall never forget one occasion when all our luggage was lost. The train, which never hurried, was very late. The only thing to do was to go straight to the hall and wait. Our accompanist was an odd-looking being who strangely resembled a donkey but he was a fine pianist. His luggage was not lost, so he was in evening dress. After we had been waiting for two hours, our dear old impresario, who had a shock of hair and a big moustache, got on the platform and after a great deal of flourishing of arms and clearing of throat, asked the audience whether they would rather wait for our luggage or would they rather have the concert now. The audience shouted 'Wait', clearly not caring if they had to wait all night. We waited too, getting hungrier and hungrier and feeling dirtier and dirtier but at last our bags arrived and on we went. Oh, how they enjoyed it.

At Debrecen we met a wonderful countess. She was very rich and lived in a beautiful castle high on a mountain. She was over seventy but a great character. She warmly invited us to supper after the concert. Everything was of the best – the finest Hungarian dishes, delicious old Tokay. After the supper chairs were cleared and we danced to her own Tzigane Band. She was the greatest dancer of us all in spite of her age. I shall never forget her picking up her skirts, showing her button boots and dancing those intricate steps with the verve of a girl of seventeen. She was a marvel and a tremendous sport. At last we went to rest, which was hardly worth it as we had to be up and on the way by four the next morning.

What fun our travels were and what a glorious city was Budapest at this time. It was here that I had the honour of meeting David Popper, a wonderful man with pure white hair and black, black eyes.* He was so delightful and enthusiastic about my cello when he entertained us at his house after a concert and I played some of his lovely pieces to him. He told me then how heartbroken he was that so many cellists, however great, always played his music as though they did not like it, and always so quickly. He then took up his cello and although elderly, played to us with all the charm possible, accompanied by his wife.

The last time I played in Budapest, I received a magnificent laurel wreath, with a tiny gold laurel wreath attached to it. It was

---

* David Popper (1843–1913), Czech virtuoso cellist and composer, a professor at the Budapest Academy from 1896, wrote many compositions for cello, including the well-known *Dance of the Elves*.

given to me by a group of students who had heard and loved the concert and I have it still amongst my greatest treasures.

I so often think of Poland. What a wonderful city Warsaw was! On our first visit a curious thing happened. As I was playing I noticed a small thin individual watching the cello as though he wanted to swallow it whole. I thought very little of it as when one is very nervous, as I was that night, things can become accentuated. We had our darling German maid with us. Mother had become a little worried at the great crowds of students who followed us everywhere, even on to the trains after concerts, so she told Elise to stay with us whenever there was a crowd around. The poor dear had never been to an orchestral concert before. The hall was absolutely crammed and the conductor was just about to raise his baton when he stopped in mid-air. We heard a scuffle and our faithful maid, who felt that this was a crowd if ever there was one, had followed us on to the platform and with her hat crooked was murmuring '*Fräulein Beatrice, wo soll ich mich setzen?*' She wanted a chair to be placed on the platform next to me! My sister told her to go but she looked so imploringly at me that I signalled to the second trombone who kindly escorted her into the wings from where she could keep her eye on us at all times!

The conductor then gave an enormous double twirl and the concert started – and what an audience it was! The *Rococo Variations* caused a sensation and the cello was recalled twenty times. Each time that young man seemed mesmerised by the cello. I quite expected to see him in the artistes' room but he did not come although many others from that enthusiastic audience did. What impressed me so much was how magnificently most of them were dressed.

We went on to Lemberg and straight to rehearsals. On the day of the concert it was pouring with rain. Our cab was very old and full of straw, the horse looked quite a hundred years old and nodded sleepily all the way to the hall, as did the driver. During the journey we passed groups of people looking like white ghosts, with sunken eyes, tall hats and dark gaberdine robes. They seemed to come from holes in the ground and from doorways and they followed our cab until we reached the artistes' entrance of the hall. There some twelve of them stood gazing at us by the light of the single oil lamp. We had to jump over a large puddle but I landed safely with the cello and as I stood waiting for a few minutes for the door to open I felt hands touching my white satin frock and saw these ghost-like people gazing at me with reverence in their eyes. They also touched the cello case but the door opened and they were pushed roughly away by the porter. I shall never forget the look in the eyes of the Jew who was looking into my eyes as he knelt at my feet, for these apparitions were Jews from the Jews' Market of Lemberg.

We went on to Paderewski's birthplace, Cracow, the great university town of Poland, full of beautiful art treasures. Once again the audiences loved the cello, enthusiasm never waned and the halls were crammed full for every performance. It did not seem to tell against us that we were English girls.

I think one of the greatest conductors was Weingartner who was one of the most courteous of men. He conducted the Schubert *Unfinished Symphony* and the Beethoven *Pastoral* when we played in Vienna again and was very anxious for us to go to supper with him afterwards. I think his conducting was something apart, something beyond this world, but he had great gaiety too. A few years afterwards he came to London but he seemed much older, probably because he had lost his beloved wife.

From Poland we went straight to Norway, where my beloved Princess Victoria was staying with her sister Queen Maud and King Haakon. They all came to our concert and in the middle I suddenly noticed that the King had a button off his boot!

The next afternoon we were invited to the Palace where we

had a heavenly time. The Queen presented us with exquisite brooches including one for Mother. I could not resist mentioning the lost boot button to the dear Princess. The King overheard our conversation and laughed. 'Yes, yes,' he said, 'it is quite true but I have had it sewn on since then.'

We were sad to leave Norway but went on to Sweden where we met Järnefelt and his wife (who was Sibelius's sister). They were both charming to us, and what a magnificent musician Järnefelt was.

Then to Denmark and back to Berlin.

When we got home to Berlin I went to hear Eugen d'Albert play at the Philharmonic Hall with Nikisch conducting. I had heard records of d'Albert and very much wanted to hear him play. He was at his zenith that night; both he and Nikisch seemed inspired. He played the Emperor Concerto, and though such a small being he seemed to have the same inner strength as the great Busoni, who was fortunate in having long fingers. I had just heard Busoni play at the house of a friend, where he would improvise by the hour. I went round to the artistes' room afterwards and d'Albert expressed the wish we might meet again some day.

I had the good fortune to meet many wonderful composers in Berlin and on my travels at this period. At the home of a French woman in Berlin (where I had heard Busoni in fact) I met Fauré one night. He had come to Berlin to hear his *Requiem* performed and as he was a great friend of the Frenchwoman, he had promised to spend the evening at her house. She asked me if I would like to play his beautiful *Elégie* with him. I jumped at the idea as I loved it and so wanted to hear how he wished it played. Fauré told me that he had composed this work in memory of his child. I was so grateful for the honour he did me by playing it with me.

That same evening eight of us danced to the strains of a small orchestra playing his *Pavane*. We all had beautiful new dresses and the occasion will always remain in my mind as a lovely vision of music and movement.

I also met Humperdinck at this house. He was a wonderful-looking man and very pleasant. We talked of his opera *Hansel and Gretel*, always one of my favourites.

A few months later we returned to England, for I was to be presented at Court, the first Court of the season. Paquin made my frock, of the most exquisite soft satin covered with Mechlin lace from my mother's own collection. The train had bunches of lilies of the valley embroidered on it and my bouquet was of the same flowers. I had such a feeling of elation when, after Mother who was presenting me had made her curtsey, I stepped forward into what seemed to be an Arabian Nights fantasy. At that Court many Rajahs were present and their jewels and the magnificence of their robes was unbelievable. The King and Queen were most gracious and I saw my beloved Princess Victoria who gave me a special smile. It really was a gala night as so many of my friends were presented with me.

On 16th June 1911 Beatrice appeared as soloist at the Queen's Hall with Sir Henry Wood. This was one of her most important concerts to date as it was effectively her début as an adult player. She played the Haydn Concerto in D, the Dvořák Concerto, and Tchaikovsky's Variations on a Rococo Theme. The critics were impressed and promised her a brilliant and glorious future. It is interesting to note that in the Haydn she used the exceedingly difficult cadenzas of Becker. A letter arrived the next day from her old teacher Mr Whitehouse:

My dear Baba,

You delighted me immensely on Friday. Your technique is magnificent – and your production of tone beautiful. I like the D and G strings of your cello but I feel the 1st string is not so good in quality. I enjoyed the Dvořák Concerto most, it was nobly played and faithfully played too. Your cadenzas in the Haydn were BEAUTIFULLY played but they are not a bit relevant! and sound as if they are 'dragged' into the work – and they are nothing to do with it! As for the one in the slow movement – it's wholly out of keeping and entirely foreign to the sentiment of the beautiful movement. You must write some yourself and use some of the themes of the work! I was intensely pleased with your playing – and consider you are quite wonderful and charming . . .

Love and earnest congratulations

W.E. Whitehouse

That summer a glorious cello came to England. It had been made in Venice by Pietro Guarnerius in 1739, the only cello ever made by him. It had been for many years in the private collection of Baron Knoop in Petrograd, in a glass case. Now it had come to London, to the firm of Messrs Hill & Co. Mr Alfred Hill asked me if I would like to see it and when I did, I knew it was the cello of my dreams. The colour was that of the setting sun and there was not a scratch or crack in it despite its age. It was a very big cello and I was told that through the making of this glorious instrument Pietro's fame became as great as that of Giuseppe Guarnerius.

Mr Alfred Hill kindly allowed me to his house or to his Bond Street shop to try the instrument, for I felt I could never leave it. Of course such an instrument was extremely costly and it was through the help of Mrs Paget who lent me some of the money and, after her death, through the utter goodness of Princess Victoria who repaid the debt to Mrs Paget's estate, that Pietro, as I called the cello, came into my possession. How I worked and how I loved all the difficulties that were given to me owing to the size of the instrument. Ordinary fingering was no good to me – I had to arrange my own, sometimes working for hours on a passage that cellists with longer fingers would have found quite easy.

The time came for us to return to Berlin, and I saw that d'Albert was playing at a Philharmonic concert. Afterwards he came to our flat and asked if I would play some Beethoven and Brahms Sonatas in Vienna and Berlin with him and then perhaps we would go next season to London. Of course this was a wonderful chance for me and I was delighted. He also wanted me to play his Cello Concerto with him conducting. This was a delightful work and he was pleased with my execution of it.

May and I then went to Leipzig. When I arrived on the platform to rehearse for the concert, I was very puzzled to find Nikisch, with a broad smile, humming to himself the first theme of Beethoven's Fifth Symphony: it suddenly dawned on me, he thought he had arranged for me to become d'Albert's fifth wife!

Another curious thing was that I noticed that thin young man there at the rehearsal. As I turned round to greet the orchestra, there at the last desk of the cellos was the same eager face of that young man. This time surely we would speak to each other. No, it was not to be, at the end of the rehearsal I looked up and he had gone.

There were a great many musicians at the concert that night and Nikisch conducted magnificently. Professor Julius Klengel was there and he urged me to work and work at the cello until I attained the greatest heights. How I enjoyed it all and how I vowed I would work.*

After the concert we went to supper with Nikisch and met the soprano Elena Gerhardt. Nikisch's eyes twinkled most of the time as he thought of d'Albert and what he was plotting. As he said goodbye he made me a bow and sang to me, his hand on his heart!

---

* Julius Klengel (1859–1933), German cellist and composer, Professor at Leipzig Conservatory, numbered Suggia, Feuermann and Piatigorsky among his pupils. He composed some interesting cello works including a *Hymn* for twelve cellos.

We left the next morning, accompanied by a railway carriage full of young students who wanted to travel a few stations with us and talk music. We had to return to Berlin for a few days to get our passports ready for Petersburg, city of my dreams. I had always longed to go to Russia and it was to come true at last. Alas, it was only to be to that one town, but never mind.

It did seem a very long and tedious journey but there were many interesting people to talk to on the train. When we arrived at the frontier it was bitterly cold but we had to get out and stand for hours while half a dozen Russians argued amongst themselves. As far as could be understood we could not enter Russia, there was something wrong with our passports. They seemed to think that the face shown in my passport was not the same as my own face! They talked and talked and tapped the cello all over. We were terribly worried and very cold.

At last I could bear it no longer. I marched up to one of the men and boldly told him that we were the nieces of Sir Edward Lugard. As the dear old General had been a hero of the Indian Mutiny and had been dead for many years and had had no connection whatsoever with Russia, I cannot imagine how I thought this would help but I was desperate. Suddenly a very stout man with a long nose approached us, pushing the passport men aside. He took off his hat, made a bow and asked if he could help us. I told him in German of our difficulties and mentioned that I had told the officials we were the nieces of Sir Edward Lugard. He gave a large wink, went straight to the customs officer and said a few words in Russian. The only thing I could under-stand were the words 'Sir Edward Grey' and then within seconds there were smiles all round and we were escorted back on the train. Our kind helper followed and told us that we were now Sir Edward Grey's nieces (I do not think the poor man had any really). He looked at us and said, 'Don't forget that this is the only way you have been able to get into Russia.' We all laughed. It seems that at that time Sir Edward Grey was very much loved by the Russians and mentioning his name had been sufficient to clear our path. We were very charmed and intrigued by our confederate who told us his name and said that he would come to our concert.

With thankful hearts we arrived at a lovely hotel. In the cold the sky was like lead and everything looked cheerless including the city which seemed quite silent and dead. Our audience, however, was anything but dead; not only were they enthusiastic but they showed the most absorbed and intelligent interest.

The rehearsal was held the morning after we arrived. May, who assured me she remembered all her Russian perfectly (she never could speak much), got into a droshky with the violin, and Mother and I got into another with the cello. I remember May wrapped her head in a white shawl and gave the address of the hall in Russian to the driver, and off she went. The droshkies were open and it was snowing hard. Our dear old horse was slow and the driver quite drunk and we had to hold on very tight. I clasped the cello while Mother tried to steady the driver with her umbrella, as he swayed from side to side. The situation was so funny that we laughed until tears ran down our cheeks, where they promptly froze. Meanwhile May's white shawl, which was a sort of beacon to us, seemed to recede further and further into the distance and our old coachman was becoming more and more difficult to hold on his seat. I was sure mother's umbrella would break when suddenly, to my joy, May's droshky stopped and I thought we had arrived. Not at all, we were lost and our cabman was fast asleep. *Et voilà*, it was proved we could not trust my sister's Russian. However, after a great deal of searching we found a programme amongst the music and we hailed a passer-by who was sympathetic and helpful. May's droshky galloped off again and I gave our old boy a whack and after one and a half hours we arrived.

Dear Glazunov was enchanted to see us again and introduced us to many great musicians including Archibuchev, Rachmaninov,

Ziloti and many others. After a time we began to rehearse. It was a great effort for Glazunov to climb up on the rostrum and I am sure he was very sleepy because the first violinist had to tap him on the arm before he began conducting. He conducted the Brahms Double Concerto very slowly – the fast and the slow movement the same!

It is interesting to note Rachmaninov's comments à propos of the first performance of his Symphony No. 1 which Glazunov conducted in 1897: 'I am amazed how such a highly talented man as Glazunov can conduct so badly. I am not speaking of his conducting technique (one can't ask that of him) but of his musicianship. He feels nothing when he conducts. It is as if he understands nothing . . .' Years later Rachmaninov's wife remarked that Glazunov was drunk at the time.

The public was wonderful and brought us back some forty times! Glazunov himself was adorable, an enormous great man of about six foot three who used the tiniest baton and made quaint little bows. After the Brahms my sister played Glazunov's own Concerto for Violin with immense success and I played his *Chant du Ménéstral* once again. In that atmosphere I felt more than ever how perfectly he had depicted the real tragedy of the old minstrel and the intense misery and hopelessness of the end. Playing it that night with Glazunov gave me a strange feeling which always lived on in my heart and soul. There was a roar of applause and Glazunov beamed all over. The audience would not stop clapping, so the pianist came back on and I played twenty-seven encores and had fifty recalls!

In Russia the cello is the King of Instruments – it is revered like the great deep Russian voices. At the very end of the concert the whole orchestra stood up and bowed with us and dear old Glazunov made a deep curtsey. I nearly died of laughter!

Afterwards many young students came and carried us shoulder-high through the hall and out to our carriage; they also carried my beloved cello shoulder-high, which gave me great joy. When we reached the carriage, they installed us gently and then took the horses from the shafts and dragged our carriage themselves to our hotel, singing wonderful Russian songs all the way. I think the Russians are the only people who clap in unison, as I have never heard it done elsewhere. What a concert that was, and how I thank God for joys such as this to have been given to me.

The next day we went to lunch with dear Glazunov and his old Mother. As she could only speak Russian we could only smile at one another. She was very stout with high cheek-bones and twinkling eyes. She wore a very tight satin blouse which I feared might burst its buttons at any minute.

We were having some wonderful Russian dishes when I fool-ishly asked Glazunov to pass me the salt. He was in a terrible state and cried, 'No, no. You will bring sorrow to this house.' I felt terrible, as though I had committed a crime. He brought in a servant who passed me the salt but I was too upset to finish my lunch, salt or no. Afterwards we did have a heavenly time and I tried to forget this incident. Glazunov took us round the Conservatoire and Professor Auer met us and talked and talked. We then had a Russian tea party and were given some exquisite icons and other presents.

When we left at least a hundred young people saw us off, shouting in English, 'Come back, come back . . .' but alas, it could never be and I did not see Russia again.

On our way back to Berlin we met our friend who had helped us to enter Russia. He told us, amongst other things, that he was an international spy! He told us that by birth he was a Polish Jew and he gave us lots of advice on many topics including cooking. We met him many times on returning home – he was a very remarkable man.

When we got back to Berlin I learned that another of my dreams was to come true. I was to play in America! Before this however I played in Vienna with d'Albert and I told him I was going to play his Concerto at my début in New York. He seemed terribly depressed and asked me, before I left, whether I would become his wife. It was an honour but I told him it was impossible (I did not add, 'to be his first, second, third, fourth or fifth wife'). However, although he said his heart was broken, it soon mended, as I heard that he later married a sixth wife before he died! I had very much enjoyed the duets with such a musical genius for Eugen d'Albert shared with me a true love of work and thought nothing of spending all day going over a difficult sonata. This was our common ground. Although a great deal, it was not enough, so after our tender farewell Mother hurried me off.

5

'Expect us on the Lusitania'

May and I returned to London triumphant, having played the Double Brahms at some fifty-nine concerts throughout Europe. I gave two recitals at the Bechstein Hall in London. One of these was with Hamilton Harty and the other with d'Albert.

Hamilton Harty was a very dear friend of the family. He began his London career as an accompanist having studied in Ireland under the Italian composer Esposito. He accompanied May and Beatrice at many of their early recitals. A letter he wrote Beatrice on 17th February 1912 contains some interesting advice:

Dear Miss Beatrice Harrison,

Generally I loathe and hate writing to anyone about anything but I want to tell you that I admire your cello playing more than anything I have heard for a long time and I think you are going to be one of the few really big artists and I am sure you will not mind if I give you two ideas that I have found very useful and helpful. One is that it seems to help one's music to take a general interest in all other artistic things like painting and books – life is not all music – and the other is not to be nervous. You may be quite sure that no matter how critical or educated an audience may be, you always know a good deal more than they – even when you are not in really good form. So the thing to do is to be calm and play

as well as you can – without being conceited, be a little proud
of your music and confident in yourself. I thought these two
bits of advice might be useful to you and I send them with
my sincere good wishes.

*Beatrice often played the compositions of Hay, as Hamilton Harty was
known to his friends, throughout her life. Later he became a well known
and well loved conductor, raising the reputation of the Hallé Orchestra as
permanent conductor between the wars.*

*Shortly after this Beatrice went abroad with Mrs Paget to Aix-les-
Bains. The sound of the cello seemed to soothe this wealthy invalid and
she loved Beatrice to play for her by the hour. She was full of plans,
inviting all the family to stay with her in the South of France before
Beatrice's American tour, planning for them to accompany her to
Vienna . . . but the idea of forming part of a wealthy woman's entourage
was not for Beatrice, as she said in a letter home.*

Aix les Bains 13 juillet 1913
    It's a funny life we lead here, sometimes I laugh until I
nearly weep to see the faces when everything goes wrong and
the twenty-five pillows are not quite right . . .

*Nevertheless Mrs Paget was very good to Beatrice and helped with the
proposed winter trip to America by preparing letters of introduction and
even lending a large sum of money to spend on advertising the tour.*

I set off for America with a trembling heart. I felt I had an import-
ant mission to perform. I was the first woman cellist to play in
Carnegie Hall and the first to be engaged to play with the Boston
Symphony Orchestra and the Chicago Symphony Orchestra.

For the Philharmonic Orchestra under Stransky at the Carnegie
Hall I wore an organdie frock trimmed with diamanté and a
wreath of red roses on my head. Fritz Kreisler and his wife were

staying at the same hotel and Mrs Kreisler was so kind, showing me how to make up for the platform. The hall was not very full as Americans were not used to a woman playing the cello. I played the d'Albert Concerto and although not every reviewer liked it, they all seemed pleased with me. One or two were more effusive in their style of review than was the custom here in England, '. . . it is impossible to believe that those sweet singers of antiquity sang a more alluring song by the summer sea than the seductive tones which Beatrice Harrison drew from her cello last Thursday night. Penelope may thank her stars that her susceptible Ulysses was not enticed by such a siren song on his journey home to Ithaca . . .'!

New York is a marvellous city. It was like fairyland when our huge liner entered the harbour and the Statue of Liberty came into view. There were thousands of lights of every shade and variety. I stood on deck and could only stare; our arrival at night seemed a meeting of heavenly stars with those on earth. Those who go by air nowadays miss such a great deal.

I had many letters of introduction and so received many private engagements. One was at a huge house the size of a palace. The husband was in business and his wife loved entertaining. They had an English butler who was most courteous – it was quite beyond my comprehension why he ever became their butler. We arrived early on the day I went to arrange my programme and he, the butler, opened the door and showed us in. A little to my surprise he then sat down and began talking about England. He then asked if I would like to play some pieces with him accompanying me on the organ in the drawing-room. I said I would be delighted and we played with all our hearts until suddenly we heard footsteps. I have never seen a man get off an organ stool so fast and disappear. The next moment our hostess entered, full of smiles and jewels, and rang for tea. Our friend the butler brought it in with an expressionless face. How strange the world is sometimes!

In Boston I played the Strauss Sonata in F, Bach's G major Suite, some Boccherini, Fauré's *Elégie* and some pieces by Hamilton Harty. The recital was a great success. I had come to America aware that the cello was not a popular instrument and so one comment above all others thrilled me after that concert. A reviewer called me a remarkable violoncellist, 'so remarkable that she may even renew a measure of public interest in her instrument and the music for it . . .' This had been my aim in bringing the cello to America. If only I could succeed.

Next I played in Chicago with dear Stock. It was there I received a heavenly bunch of Malmaison roses from Claire Dux, whom I had last seen in *Der Rosenkavalier* in Dresden some years before.

I also received several offers of marriage and one quite nice man, somewhat lacking in sense of humour, offered me his heart and his banking account. I should not have minded the bank account but the heart I could not cope with, so had to refuse both! He remained a kind friend however and revered the cello. More and more it was a surprise and a delight to me to see how my cello was loved wherever I played. The people got over their prejudice at seeing and hearing a woman play this instrument. Of course personality means a great deal in America and as I loved my audiences they seemed to love me in return and I am sure that nowhere else is an artiste revered as in America. It makes no difference if one is a newcomer, if one is offering the best and only the best they will understand it. The press had been kind to me throughout the trip and I left feeling the cello had been truly appreciated.

I did not make a very long tour but before I left I went to play at the White House. The President at the time was Woodrow Wilson, such a gentle and delightful man and very appreciative. In memory of the visit he gave me a beautiful gold brooch. A few days later I celebrated my 21st birthday. How very lucky and happy I was!

We returned to Europe and I fulfilled some continental engagements before the war broke out. I was excited to hear that my success in America had resulted in my being engaged for a second tour, a really big one.

Before this however another event occurred which was to prove of great importance in our lives. May and I were invited to play the Brahms Double Concerto with the Hallé Orchestra under Beecham, at Manchester. At the end of the performance an elegant gentleman rushed up to us full of charm and enthusiasm and introduced himself to us as Frederick Delius. He told us that he was going to write a Double Concerto for us himself and this was a great thrill indeed. We subsequently became close friends and in fact some of his great works were composed in our garden at home.

In spite of the war I was able to fulfil my engagements in America. Mother, May and Monica came with me, leaving only Father and Margaret at home. It was a very big tour covering a great deal of the West. There the German-speaking immigrants were as good to me and my cello as if there had been no war.

My agent told me on arrival that it was very unwise to bring my sister out as accompanist but I found afterwards that he was entirely wrong. I later learned that the public would have been much more thrilled had May played under her own name. But no, it had to be Marie Smith, and oh, the fun we had! So many people looked at May and then at me and said, 'I know you are sisters by the way she plays for you.' There was nothing to say, we smiled broadly.

The tour went well and we were looking forward to seeing our dear ones again.

In London, however, Colonel Harrison was worried about their return. In a letter to his wife dated 10th March 1915 he says, 'Even the big liners are not free from German agents, but no doubt you know more of this than we do as the report emanated from Washington.' (In fact they

*knew nothing of this and little dreamed how very first-hand their experi-
ence of 'German agents' was shortly to become.) Colonel Harrison wrote
again on 30th March 1915:*

> Today's papers bring news of a most dastardly act on the
> part of the German submarines. Two liners have been
> torpedoed – passenger ships – on the West coast of England
> and many lives lost . . . in a brutal and callous manner the
> crew of the submarines being said to have laughed and jeered
> at the poor drowning people . . .

*Poor Colonel Harrison, alone with his youngest daughter, was very anxious
indeed: 'This makes all of us here think it would be better if you postponed your departure.'*

We were to sail from New York on our return from Chicago and
my sister May particularly wanted to sail on the *Lusitania*. We
knew some of the officers and they had promised us a wonderful
time and I had been asked to do a concert on board, in aid of
the Sailors' Home. So it was arranged and mother cabled Father
to expect us on the *Lusitania*. Two nights before the ship was due
to sail I remember my mother rising from her bed and walking
up and down the room. She was not at all happy – she had had
an awful premonition – she saw a terrible shipwreck, but of which
ship she could not tell. The next day however, she telephoned and
cancelled our passages although May almost wept with disappointment. There was no other ship due to sail immediately and friends
who were going on the *Lusitania* were highly amused but Mother
remained firm. At last a little old American liner was scheduled
to sail and we took passage in that ship.

Mother had already cabled Father to expect us on the *Lusitania*
and although she sent him another cable telling him of our change
of plans, he never received it.

The little ship was so crowded that the only cabins we could secure were two small inner ones into which we had to fit a hundred pieces of luggage as well as ourselves. My cabin was so small that it was almost a cupboard and it admitted no air or light except through a running slit at ceiling level into the next cabin, which was an outside one.

The first night we felt too tired to think or speak. It was spring time and very warm and airless and we fell into a heavy sleep. The next night however, at about midnight, waking with a start, I heard someone continuously tearing papers in the cabin next door. I felt I must know more so I woke May and together we listened. At last I asked her in a whisper if I could climb on her shoulders as I wished to put one eye to the slit in the wall and see what was happening. With much difficulty I got up and lo and behold, there was a small dark man surrounded by papers which he was taking from a case labelled 'Hotel Adler', one of the largest hotels in Berlin. I hopped down as poor May was collapsing with my weight. The next night however, the same thing happened and as I watched the cabin door opened stealthily and another man put his head round the door and was beckoned in by his confederate. They had a long talk in German, every word of which of course I understood, and then the second man left. It was about three o'clock in the morning but there was no sleep for us, we had to tell Mother and she was as worried as we were.

During the day there was absolute peace, as the man and his companions evidently rested. That night a third man crept in and they held a meeting and every night they laid their plans, little thinking that anyone was listening, let alone the two musicians, daughters of an English Colonel, who all the while were gleaning information in German and writing it down. How we hoped and prayed that the information we were obtaining would help our beloved country.

It took the little *St Louis* three weeks to cross the Atlantic, dodging the mines laid by the enemy. One night while we were dining I remember that we heard of the terrible tragedy of the *Lusitania*. It made our blood run cold for an instant as we gazed at our beloved Mother.

When we were about three nights off land, my sister and I climbed on top of the luggage which we had piled on my bunk and after listening for a few minutes to the conversation taking place in the next cabin we knew for sure that the two men were spies. They were arranging to meet other confederates at a certain date in Berlin. We felt very anxious but Mother insisted that we go to the Captain and report all that we had heard. He listened to us with great interest and was delighted with all the details we were able to furnish him with; there had been other suspicions that these men were German spies and now he was sure of it. The last night, as we listened, we heard one man say to the other, 'Now all is ready, we shall meet on the thirteenth of May.' We noticed that this particular man had grown a beard during the voyage to try to disguise himself.

The landing of our luggage in Liverpool was colossal. We had Japanese trees as well as the hundred cases. Our poor old steward was English and very short-tempered. He had tried to get into the army but had failed as he had flat feet and was over-age. This time he vented his anger on us, the passengers with the most luggage. I have never before or since heard such swear-words, but Mother was sorry for him and gave him a double tip.

At last we got off and went straight to the phone, as Mother felt in her bones that Father had not received the cable. She was right and when she got through Father almost wept with relief and joy. He had gone through torture thinking that we were all on the *Lusitania*.

We had a heavenly welcome from Margaret and Father and for a time forgot the spies until, some months later, we read in the paper of two individuals who had travelled from New York on the American liner *St Louis* and who had been taken by the police from Liverpool and incarcerated in the Tower!

There was a very sad feeling about England at this time and we felt it deeply, although we had no brothers. So many of our childhood friends and so many of the sons of Father's brother officers were killed. Many others were wounded including Bunt Goschen although he, happily, recovered fully. Others were not so fortunate and it was awful to see so many young men physically maimed or suffering from shattered nerves. The only thing I could do was to try to give some peace to them with my music.

I particularly remember one concert we gave at the Queen's Hall with the Royal Engineers' Band, in aid of comforts for Father's regiment. Queen Alexandra gave her kind patronage and came to the concert with our beloved Princess Victoria. I am happy to say it was a great success and brought in plenty of money.

We had to rearrange our big town house so that we could sleep downstairs in the safest part. This meant making the rooms upstairs into a dining-room and kitchen and we had a peculiar lift arranged with a rope so that we could get downstairs in a hurry.

Mother had a marvellous time with her little oven, placed in what had been Father's dressing-room. She used to make remarkable dishes for the wives of the troops who came to help and whenever a bomb dropped there was a cake in the oven. All were given a great deal of sympathy as well as lovely food for Mother had an incredible ability to make the most of any situation and to bring others through it with her. She also made us laugh a lot.

Uncle Charles was Commandant at the Millbank Military Hospital. One afternoon when we were at tea, the phone rang and Mother answered it. She rushed back very white in the face. 'John,' she cried, 'your dear brother has had a bomb six feet long dropped on him.' 'The dear boy', as we and the Princess always called him, looked puzzled at this ballistic impossibility. 'No, six inches, you mean, not six feet.' Mother insisted so father went to the telephone and returned with a smile. 'Six inches,' was all he said. (Uncle was unharmed.)

So the sad days wore on. There were pageants, concerts and heartbreaks. What a strange and terrible feeling of desolation that war gave one and what a great pleasure it was to hear that in America a fresh tour had been planned and that all my friends were looking forward to seeing me again.

I was to tour with Dame Nellie Melba. The tour began in Toronto and it was wonderful to feel the absolute loyalty of the Canadians to Britain. I did not meet Melba until just before the first concert when I arrived at the hall. Girls were strewing beautiful flowers on the ground for her to walk through. After I had been introduced, I told her how much she must be loved for the people to do this. She looked at me with a steely eye – 'You fool,' she said, 'don't you know that I pay for this myself? Where are your brains?' This was my introduction to Madame Melba but I must say she was very honest to tell me this!

The tour covered a great part of the United States. Naturally Melba loved admiration and her voice was still as pure as crystal. (As Mother, writing home to Monica who was training as a singer, said, 'We heard Melba practising scales and arpeggios and trills last evening . . . her art is very fine, her glissandos are perfectly exquisite and her attack is magnificent but her poor maid has rather a trying time, I never saw anyone get angry quite so suddenly as Madame M . . .')

On one occasion someone unknown to me sent a heavenly bouquet. I was charmed, but the manager came rushing up to me in a terrible state. 'You cannot have that bouquet handed to you unless I can purchase a larger one for Madame Melba – remember that!' He flew out to see if he could procure one for her and came back thankfully with a huge one, so I was able to receive mine. That was Madame Melba in Chicago.

We went on to New York and the concert in Carnegie Hall was crammed. Melba was in her gala clothes – tiara and all. I had just opened the programme with one of Handel's most lovely sonatas, then the tenor sang, but where was Melba? I went to her dressing-room and found Melba and my dear Mother having a terrible tussle. It took me several horrified minutes to grasp what was happening. Melba's corset was too tight and Mother, in bending forward to help her loosen it, had entangled a beautiful aigrette in her hat with Melba's tiara! They rocked backwards and forwards – Mother in helpless laughter, Melba in hopeless anger. At last I helped them to put things right and the concert proceeded and was a huge success.

Melba was never gracious to the cello, which hurt me very deeply. Sometimes however, I had more success than she did, which made her very angry, but what could I do? However, she was always very honest and at the end of the tour she was gracious enough to say that I should have been her co-artiste, which was very generous of her.

It was soon after this that I met two people who were to become our lifelong and very dear friends. One was Mary Hillier ('Hillie') who had a passion for all things English and who would lay down her life for anyone from England, and the other was Mrs Sydney Thayer who came up to me after the Carnegie Hall concert with her arms extended and with whom all my subsequent American tours were wrapped up. She was a great musician and a great music critic and she has been everything to me, supporting us with loving letters and throughout the Second World War, food parcels and moral support.

It was 1916, so back at home I played at Red Cross concerts at hospitals. My sisters were all doing the same and even Monica was now singing and appearing in pageants for fund-raising for war charities.

Delius, by now a dear friend, had completed the Concerto for Violin and Cello for us although it was to be some years before we played it in public. The strange thing was that it was written in unison and technically was almost impossible to play but with Delius himself and Peter Heseltine at the piano, we rewrote the cello part and made it playable. Delius sat for hours with a large cushion and the score on his knees, surrounded by four of our Scottie dogs, who took a great interest in the proceedings and periodically licked his fingers which made him jump, throw everything in the air and have to begin again. Heseltine banged out the orchestral part, while I, hot and anxious, played each passage over and over again until Delius was satisfied that it corresponded perfectly with the violin. All this took weeks but at last it was finished. Delius would have liked me to play it in America as music in Europe was in a poor state because of the war. He thought that he himself might come to America the following year with us but meanwhile he gave me several names and addresses of friends in the musical world in America. I had for some time been urging him to write me something for cello and orchestra and before I left he promised me that he would try to do so.

We eventually sailed for the States and when we reached New York Mother and I went to a tiny hotel in Seventh Avenue as we were anxious to spend as little money as possible on ourselves. Before leaving England I had been feeling terribly ill, but that was no time for personal aches and pains. By the time we arrived however, I almost collapsed and felt dreadfully snappy.

I had to work very hard, as I had only ten days to work up a whole new programme. The day of my first concert arrived and I awakened with my face and body practically black. It then occurred to me that I must have caught an awful type of jaundice that was then raging in England. I was also as thin as could be but what to do? Our chambermaid, a black girl, was worried too and said, half-jokingly, that we looked like twins. This shocked Mother into rushing out and buying what she called 'white paint' but which was really liquid powder.

I had an exquisite dress, pearl-grey satin with a large collar, and at last with my face, neck, chest, arms, hands and fingers thickly coated with the liquid powder, I was ready. How handsome I must have looked, for the jaundice very quickly began to show through the white powder.

The concert was in aid of the Red Cross and was packed. As I began the beautiful Bach Chorale which Anthony Bernard,* whom I had met in England, had arranged for me, I felt as though I was in a dream and I could hardly see the audience. It was really quite a delicious sensation, for all pain had left me and I was as if dreaming. I was however brought back to earth somewhat when I noticed that the liquid powder was coming off and that I was half white, half bruised-looking yellow!

After the concert I hastily put on my coat before receiving the many kind people who came to talk to me. Amongst them was a doctor and he came straight to the point. 'Do you know you are drunk with fever?' he asked. I told him I did feel queer and he asked if he could take my temperature. It was 105°. The doctor was Jewish and very brilliant and he became one of the cello's greatest friends. He said he could never understand how I managed to get through that concert and play as I did with a temperature of 105°. The concert was a great success, which was most important, and it raised a large sum of money for the Fund. The Press too were very kind and so I felt happy.

I returned to the small hotel, and with the help of my doctor friend became my usual colour in time for another great concert in Boston. After this our kind friends invited Mother and me

---

* Anthony Bernard (1891–1963), organist, piano accompanist and conductor, founded the London Chamber Orchestra and Singers in 1921, and revived much old music.

to their lovely home in Philadelphia to rest. Before leaving America however, I had the privilege of playing at an afternoon 'At Home' given by a very wonderful woman living in Washington. She was so rich that it really made me thankful to be poor. She was an angel of mercy to our troops during the war. She was stout with a beaming, rosy face and the kindest eyes. She was wearing a marvellous dress resplendent with sequins and diamonds, and she had a shawl of real pearls which fell into the soup! Her hat was very heavy, and trimmed with emeralds and rubies so that it was very difficult for her to move her head. Her smile, however, was a joy to watch and she was very enthusiastic. One could hardly grasp what the treasures she possessed were worth and the room was so laden with them that some had to be nailed to the ceiling.

On returning to New York I met Paderewski again. I had met him once in London and had loved his courtesy and charm. He was always good to me and was doing great work for the Polish refugees.

He and his wife asked me to help them at the big bazaar they were running for this cause. It all went well until Madame Sembrich, who was a lifelong enemy of Madame Paderewski, appeared.* Poor Paderewski was standing between the two ladies when one of them suddenly picked up a doll and shied it at the other with great violence. Battle royal began with both ladies shrieking at each other in Polish and everyone looking on. It was a remarkable sight, with Paderewski standing between them with his eyes tight shut.

At his recitals for the Poles he always had one of the rag dolls sitting at the tail end of the piano. At his last concert at the

---

* The Polish soprano Marcella Sembrich (1858–1935) was considered one of the finest coloratura singers in the world. She was a colourful and many-talented woman. At the last night of her first season at the New York Met, she gave a display of piano-playing, violin-playing and singing, one after the other.

Carnegie Hall he took this doll and presented it to me as I sat, enraptured, in the front row. I kept her always with me, increasingly dishevelled but her wide-open blue eyes still shining.

Before we left, our kind friends gave us hundreds of boxes of candies to hand round to the men at different hospitals and so, laden with these and other gifts, we said good-bye to the States once again.

As so many boats had been torpedoed, we sailed in the very slow old liner the *Philadelphia* which took nearly three weeks to cross the Atlantic. We were in the middle of the ocean when the danger signal sounded and we learned that German torpedoes were coming full tilt towards our little steamer. The passengers were told to put on their lifebelts but there was no panic, in fact all was quiet.

I had just come in from the dining-room where I had been playing at a concert put on by the Red Cross. As I came into our cabin I found my mother sitting with about seventy women from Canada. They were both inside and outside the cabin just listening as Mother talked to them and tried to give them faith and courage. I sat down next to Mother trying to tie a life-belt round the cello but it was no good, I was ordered to put it on myself. I implored our funny old steward to give me another life-belt for the cello and with an affable smile he did so. We sat all night while mother talked to those dear souls, Mother with her life-belt on, I with mine, the cello with his. They were the wives of some of the Canadian soldiers who were allowed to come and be with their husbands before they went to the Front. They called Mother 'The Faith Healer'.

I felt very strongly that we should be saved as I was born with a caul. Sailors are always happy to have an individual born with a caul on board as that means that the sea will not drown them. Anyhow, at last we arrived safely.

It was lovely going round the hospitals with the candies from

America. I played more than once at my uncle's Military Hospital at Millbank but shortly after our return he left this hospital where he was Commandant as he had been asked to reorganise a large hospital for the American Government at Etaples. He had a beautiful little chapel built which was opened by the King and Queen and he was called the 'Guardian' of the hospital. I shall never forget the change in him when he came home; he had gone away an upright figure and returned quite bent.

After the war a choir of about sixty men with glorious voices came over from Czechoslovakia to give concerts in England. My Mother kept open house for artistes in those days, British or otherwise, and this particular choir wished to use our drawing-room for a concert. They were to travel by underground as far as Gloucester Road and there were to be met by Father. He objected at first and was very worried about the arrangements and kept murmuring, 'How shall I ever know them?' He was told to stand on the other side of the road and when sixty gentlemen of different sizes came out of the underground, to hail them and marshal them home. Not one of them spoke English but the principal tenor spoke German!

After a while I went on to the balcony and saw my dear Father, as though he were at the head of his troops, marching along followed by a miscellany of large and small, thin and stout Czech gentlemen, each wearing a trilby hat. They arrived and sang gloriously and were so enthusiastic. After we had given them refreshments, wine and beer, they made to leave us, with many kisses on the hand. When they reached the hall, there was consternation. All their hats had been put one on top of the other and they were all alike! Hearing the terrific discussions we leant over the banisters and could not help laughing; a tiny man wore a hat that was almost down to his chin, behind him a large man with a hat like a pea on the top of his head. They shouted at the husband of our housemaid, such a nice man, who had unfortunately muddled their hats but at last all was well and Father shepherded them back. At the entrance to the underground he shook hands sixty times and quite a crowd gathered to watch.

At this time we often had musicians come to the house to make music, sometimes until the early hours of the morning. Father never joined in these parties; he was slightly deaf and never quite understood musicians. One night our friend Roger Quilter and our dear friend Maude Valérie White were there. I had been playing for hours and it was four o'clock in the morning when suddenly the drawing-room door opened and my Father came in. He looked around with his gentle smile and said, 'May I ask what time is breakfast?' We looked up and Maud Valérie White rose and said to Mother, 'I have never been asked to make my departure in such a gracious way!'

Father was nervous of musicians and composers as a whole and when Mother used to tell him that she hoped we would become fine musicians he said in an apologetic manner, 'Yes, Annie dear, but it seems to me music brings forth lunatics.' Mother laughed and said, 'But John, I hope you don't consider your daughters lunatics.' 'Oh, no,' he would say, 'No, of course not,' but he sounded a little dubious. Nevertheless he took a tremendous interest in our careers and often said to me before a concert, 'Remember you are a servant of the public. Do your best, your very best, whether there are thousands in the audience or only one person and always strive to reach your ideal.'

We then had to pick up the threads of our lives once more and we often had the joy and the honour of going to Marlborough House to play with our beloved Princess Victoria. What heavenly music we made together, for she was a beautiful pianist and her knowledge of music was amazing. Very often Queen Alexandra would come in. Sometimes she was accompanied by her sister, the Dowager Empress of Russia. It was there that we first met our friend the Baroness de Stoeckl, the authoress.

At about this time the family went to Sandringham to spend a holiday with Princess Victoria, the first of several trips. They stayed at the near-by village of Dersingham during the month of September. These are a few of Beatrice's diary entries made at the time.

18th September 1918. Went all over Appleton* with Princess Victoria.

20th September. She took us over the grounds at Sandringham and showed us her own rooms. Perfectly lovely.

21st September. The Queen showed us her boudoir and bedroom, a perfect dream, all so lovely and never to be forgotten.

23rd September. The Queen showed Mother her room. Very, very sad – the spirit of King Edward pervades all. Terrible news from Russia.** Played with dear Princess in the sunset, she is so dear to us, as ever.

24th September. Princess came to fetch us this morning and we drove over the grounds, through 'Princesses Drive' to see over the little chapel. Memorials to King Edward and Prince Eddy so beautiful. Afterwards we walked round Appleton and then to see the Stud and

---

* Princess Victoria's sister Maud, Queen of Norway, who was always very homesick for England, had been given a house at Appleton, near Sandringham, by the Prince of Wales to use as a holiday residence.

**News had been received of the death of Queen Alexandra's nephew, Czar Nicholas and his family at Ekaterinburg, but the Queen was still desperately worried about her sister Dagmar (Marie Fyodorovna), the Dowager Empress, who had fled to the Crimea. Although communications had almost broken down, the Queen wrote frequently and urgently begging her to leave but it was not until 1919 that a British warship went to rescue her.

saw the successor of Persimmon named Friar's Marcus.
Then saw stable and Princess's sweet ponies, 'Dawn' and
'Kimbie'. Such a wonderfully beautiful morning – sun
and blue sky but all somehow very sad and autumn-
like.

27th September. Went up to Sandringham, had most lovely
time. The Queen presented us with exquisite presents.
She looked so sweet and young. The presents such a
surprise. Played with Princess for the last time there.
Brahms Requiem, glorious sunset, all so beautiful,
Princess simply beloved and sweet. Saw some of the
treasures in the drawing-room again. Said good-bye to
the dear Queen and old C.K. [Charlotte Knollys, lady
of the bedchamber. In fact this was not the last visit to
Sandringham.]

28th September. Princess came down in the morning on
her bicycle. Played and chatted and bid us good-bye.
Very, very sad. King and Queen M. arrived at York
Cottage. Bustle and to-do, all busy. Lovely though
bitterly cold day. Longing to see Princess again.

29th September. Went up to Sandringham. Played in dear
Princess's room upstairs. The Queen came in for a little
and Princess Mary and Lady Mary Trefusis and
Marquise d'Hautpoule were there. Princess Mary sang.
Curious voice! Played lots on two pianos. The Queen
asked us again for the next day.

30th September. Last day at Dersingham. The Princess came
in morning once more on her bike, only saw her for a
minute. In the afternoon went for final visit to
Sandringham. Played in the ball-room. Everyone there.
Queen, our Princess, Princess Mary, old C.K., Lady M.
Trefusis, Marquise d'Hautpoule, Mother, Sir Dighton
Probyn, Sir Arthur Davidson. Played lots. All so sweet

and kind. Queen gave us each (Mother and me) small
photos. So sad to leave dear Princess so beloved. Said
good-bye to all. Glorious news from the front –
Bulgarians throw up arms. Wet bitterly cold day. Such a
wonderful month. Good night.

6

Delius and Elgar

Delius had kept his promise and written something for the cello; it was his heavenly Cello Sonata which he did me the great honour of dedicating to me and which I brought out at the Wigmore Hall in October 1918. Since then I have played it all over the Continent and America, always with the same success.

In December 1918, Margaret Harrison made her début as a violinist at the Wigmore Hall. She played two movements of Bach's Sonata in A minor for Unaccompanied Violin, Debussy's Violin Sonata, and gave the first performance of Stanford's Irish Concertino for Violin and Cello, in which she was joined by Beatrice. Hamilton Harty accompanied and the whole concert was very well received. The family were delighted that Margaret had joined the ranks of professional musicians and with the ending of the war a feeling of peace and happiness pervaded the family and their circle.

We went for a delightful holiday on a farm in Devon. The farmer and his wife were so jolly and hospitable. Our greatest thrill was making butter. Margaret became most adept at it and how delicious it was. Oh, the cream and the strawberries too, what feasts we used to have! When we left Margie asked if she might take two hens back to London with her and she did, with much clucking on the journey. We kept them outside at the back of the house and they looked very comfortable but one adored roaming and

Margaret was for ever rushing round Cornwall Gardens looking for Lucia, as she was called. On one occasion the telephone rang and it was the husband from next door, asking mother severely if her daughter could come and retrieve her hen as she had just laid an egg on their grand piano! Off hopped Margaret and returned in triumph with Lucia under her arm and a beautiful warm egg in her hand which she presented to our friend and great composer of songs, Roger Quilter. He accepted with gratitude and much laughter; he had such a lovely sense of humour. It was always such a delight to play his divine songs accompanied by him on the piano. He also made some beautiful transcriptions of old melodies, one of which has been in my programme for years [*L'Amour de Moy*]. I have played it throughout America, in most of the capitals of Europe and all over England and he has been asked by many to have it published but he never would.

On 21st February 1920, at long last May and Beatrice gave the first performance of the Delius Double Concerto for Violin and Cello with Sir Henry Wood at the Queen's Hall. Delius came over for the performance which was a great success. The critics appreciated the beauty and originality of the work at once. The Times *critic stated:*

Delius is most attractive in the world of Dreams . . . the beauty of the instrumental colour with which the ideas are clothed and the opportunities it gives for an intimate ensemble between the soloists and the orchestra are things which should give the Concerto a definite place among the very few of its class which exist.

About this time we had to leave London because Mother could not stand the fogs as she had developed severe bronchitis. We took a delightful old farmhouse called The Waffrons, near Thames Ditton in Surrey. It was here that Delius and his darling wife Jelka came on a visit at Easter time and here, in the garden, that he began to compose his Cello Concerto. It was on Good Friday, one of the most perfect spring mornings I remember, and as Delius sat in the garden he was literally bathed in the golden sunlight among the flowers; the bluebells, the violets and above all the flower he loved so well, the Gloire de Dijon rose, the very earliest to breathe its perfume. Delius seemed to steep himself in its fragrance. The crystal air was vibrating with the chant of many birds, the skylark floating upwards to the clouds in an unseen world, the white doves beating their wings through the air, the blackbird, the robin, the thrush, the tiny tits, even the little jenny wren, all seemed to vie with each other to charm him.

The orchestration is most lovely and subtle. This concerto is the last orchestral work which Delius composed and it commences full of virility and joy, continuing with a slow movement which for sheer beauty of orchestral sound must surely be unexcelled in the whole range of modern music. Towards the close of the work an echo of regret seems to foreshadow his approaching blindness. Did he perhaps faintly realise that all that riot of colour he was so enraptured with in the garden would only become a memory?

The recollection of this spring morning lived on in the minds of the Deliuses no less than the Harrisons. As Jelka wrote in a letter a couple of years later:

It is strange, I could never hear the Cello Concerto without thinking of you – it is so bound up with those lovely spring days with you all at The Waffrons and this intense wish of yours and mine, that he should compose a Cello Concerto. And when he wrote it, it sounded so heavenly and flowed on and on without a break until it was finished. I felt it must be beautiful.

We went to stay with Delius and Jelka quite often after this. I wish I could describe his lovely place at Grez, near Fontainebleau, which once belonged to Robert Louis Stevenson, who left such a delightful description of the village that I cannot do better than quote it: 'It lies out of the forest, a cluster of houses with an old bridge and an old castle in ruins, and a quaint old church. The Inn garden descends in terraces to the river, stable yard, orchard and a space of lawn fringed with rushes and embellished with a green arbor. On the opposite bank there is a reach of English-looking plain, set thickly with willows and poplars. And between the two lies the river, clear and deep and full of reeds and floating lilies. Water plants cluster about the lower bridge and stand half way upon the piers in green luxuriance. They catch the dipped oar with long antennae, and chequer the slimy bottom with the shadow of their leaves. And the river wanders hither and thither among the islets and is smothered and broken up by the reeds, like an old building in the hardy arms of climbing ivy.'

Delius almost lived in his garden behind the house, or in his boat on the river in summer. He listened to the birds and I am sure that he heard glorious music from the invisible air as it wafted around him. Jelka always went with him and described to him the different lights and shades of the flowers. He had quite a passion for flowers.

Delius had a wonderful charm and his sympathy was great. In spite of his later physical disability he took a keen interest in everything going on in the outer world. He delighted in the gramophone Mother gave him (and giving was her greatest joy) as it linked him with performances of his music which he was unable to attend. Another time I gave him a Hartz Roller canary and a Chinese Nightingale. He called the canary 'Tommy' after Beecham, and he really sang divinely. Delius was always most courteous. I remember on one occasion we were late for lunch, the train was behindhand and although Delius was at that time very ill, he insisted on waiting lunch for us and then ordering his very best wine to be brought up from the cellars.

The wine had an interesting tale to tell. Just before the time when he and Jelka were forced to flee from their house and from the Germans in the 1914 war, he buried this most excellent old wine under the earth and, wonderful to relate, the Germans never found it and upon his return it was dug up intact.

The time was drawing near for Beatrice to give the first performance of Delius's Cello Concerto in London. The first performance ever was given by a young Russian cellist, Alexandre Barjansky, on 31st January 1923 in Vienna, and he gave a second performance in celebration of Delius's sixtieth birthday at Frankfurt. Jelka Delius, who appears very taken with Barjansky, writes to Adine O'Neill on 30th March 1923:

> Beatrice Harrison I am sure knows it to perfection and she would love to play it in London . . . the Phil. could do it with Barjanksy, who is sure to have a huge success. He looks extraordinary when he plays, so ecstatic with a delicate, sensitive face and hair like an Italian primitive – people would love him . . .

This apparent disloyalty to Beatrice is rectified by Delius himself. At the end of the letter Jelka says: 'I read this to Fred and he thinks Beatrice Harrison ought to play it if the Philhar. gives the Concerto.'

Very soon after this Beatrice was able to write to say that it was arranged and that she would play the Cello Concerto in London. Jelka wrote:

> Your dear enthusiastic letter arrived today and gave us the greatest pleasure. Delius said: 'I know she will play it beautifully!' How splendid that it is really to come off, and with Goossens conducting – alas, we shall not be able to come to London,

but we hope to come in September. It will be a grand concert
I hope, and apart from the great joy of our hearts, this beloved
Concerto, I hope you too will have all outward success. Delius
says of course you are to play those opening chords pizzicato,
if you prefer. He had never intended to put metronome marks
but Barjansky, who played so awfully well, has a tendency to
play too fast, so he thought to give an idea of the tempi. He
says you have always known how to take his tempi.

*Beatrice gave the first English performance of the Cello Concerto at the
Queen's Hall on 3rd July 1923. She comments:*

Eugene Goossens conducted it for me most beautifully but
I was very nervous. It is curiously written for the cello
but I think the theme of the Adagio one of the most
exquisite fragments he has written.

*Beatrice later wrote of this work in an article 'From the Performer's Point
of View' which was published in the* Musical Bulletin *in August 1927.*

Delius makes so manifest in his music the richness, fullness
and loveliness of Nature, that the player is consumed with
the desire to respond to the emotion. This love and almost
passion for nature, this miraculous power and understanding
of her and perfect sympathy with her, is greatly intensified
in this Concerto. In the opening chords one feels the herald
of Spring, which gives that intense thrill and joy that no
other season of the year can give, when the sun vibrates
through the earth and the sky has that radiant clearness that
makes one's very heart leap for joy, and the whole earth
seems full of passionate blossoming. After this comes a simple
flowing melody which fills one with heartsease. The song
of the bird pervades the whole atmosphere of the work,

sometimes full of the joy of spring, sometimes, it would seem, of regret for a past which can never return. For again that strange mystic shadow creeps into the music which is so true to nature, as in all spring-joy there is a foreshadowing of the autumn and its dying beauty and fading leaves. There is in all Delius's music that spiritual emotion which the performer must feel, and which has been well expressed in the following lines:

'. . . that serene and blessed mood,
In which the affections gently lead us on,
Until, the breath of this corporeal frame
And even the motion of our human blood
Almost suspended, we are laid asleep
In body, and become a living soul:
While with an eye made quiet by the power
Of harmony, and the deep power of joy
We see into the life of things.'

Certainly this work requires much time, thought and contemplation; as with all great art, its beauties are only reached by intense love and patience. The honour and glory is attained when the artist can convey the message that Delius speaks throughout the work.

In playing the Concerto the soloist has to realise that his part does not predominate but should weave its way through the exquisite harmonies of the orchestra, almost like a beautiful river passing through a lovely landscape ever flowing on, sometimes clear and sometimes in shadow, but ever conscious of the rhythm of the work which seems in the end to vibrate into eternity. The artist's conception of this Concerto must be an emotional one. Joy and sadness are so intermingled and the moods vary so exquisitely that it is only by understanding these transcending beauties that Delius's music can be interpreted. So mysteriously and so delicately are the harmonies interwoven that the ear must be attuned to the most sensitive degree to catch their mystic beauties. The artist must be inspired by a wealth of musical imagination to be able to interpret this music. It would seem almost impossible to describe this wonderful work adequately: for me it has been one of the greatest joys to strive to interpret it and I still hope one day to come a little nearer to the ideal.

The rest of the programme of that concert of 3rd July 1923 was extremely interesting. There were two short pieces by Goossens, the first performance of The Happy Forest *by Bax and the Elgar Cello Concerto conducted by Elgar.*

My association with Elgar at this time was, musically speaking, one of the high-points of my life. I had heard that Elgar had composed a Cello Concerto which had had its first performance at the Queen's Hall in 1919. Although Elgar himself had conducted it and Felix Salmond had brought it out, it had little success then, owing it was said to lack of rehearsals. I had never met Sir Edward, although May had played to him as a child, and so I was particularly delighted when I heard that Sir Edward would like me to make some records of his Concerto with HMV at Hayes. I loved the work with its sudden changes of mood and its grandeur.

Before making the records, I went with Margaret to his beautiful house and met him and Lady Elgar, who was so gentle and sympathetic with us. Margaret had worked hard at the piano score of the Concerto but she had played only a little of it when Sir Edward swept her off the piano stool and played it himself with great élan, poor Margie meekly turning the pages.

The day came for me to meet Sir Edward at Hayes.* We arrived early and wasn't I nervous! I waited at least two hours and at last Sir Edward and Lady Elgar arrived in a hired car. During their journey to Hayes the petrol tank of their car had burst and the filthy oil had run all over the score and parts. Poor Sir Edward, he was nearly weeping! The score was dried but the smell was still terrible and the atmosphere was one of gloom and with this mood upon us all the recording sounded dull. Oh dear, I was worried!

While I was making the records Lady Elgar sat next to Mother and after they were finished, she turned to Mother and said, 'I think your child will make people love this work when she has an opportunity of playing in public.'

Sir Edward was pleased and the next day Beatrice received a note from him.

I hope you are not too tired after yesterday: recording is rather an ordeal. I wanted to send a word of thanks to you for your beautiful playing and also for your patience . . .

Of course I still studied a great deal. One of my dearest friends who helped me almost more than any professor was dear Rubio. He was a great friend of Casals and he used to come to our little flat by the hour. I loved playing the Bach Suites with him. He was such a great artist and such a character.

---

* An example of Beatrice's compressing several events into one. The first recording session took place on 22nd December 1919, the second, which according to Elgar's diary involved the 'petrol-smelly car', should have been on 24th February 1920, but the session in which the Adagio was finished did not take place until 16th November 1920.

The fun of Rubio's personality comes over clearly in his letters to Beatrice.

My very dear Babina,

I was thinking you do not like me any more! such a long time without a line! Merci beaucoup de votre charmante lettre; je vous envoie tous mes voeux les meilleurs pour le nouvel an, dont j'en suis sûr vous aurez toute sorte de succès car vous avez de quoi le mériter, ma chère Baba.

Ayez la bonté de souhaiter *à tous* chez vous de ma part tout le bonheur imaginable pour la nouvelle année.

Je suis très heureux d'entendre que le tourte [a make of bow] vous va bien, c'est une excellente baguette pleine de la fluida de notre chèr Casals.

Je suis désolé de vous avoir manqué au Philharmonique. Il y avait aussi tout près de moi une élève à moi, Miss Baker que je n'ai pas vu *non plus!* Je ne pouvais voir autre chose que Casals. Une chanteuse qui était à côté de moi m'a parlé tout le temps sans me connâitre que de loin.

Auf *bald* wiedersehen Liebe *Babanskindstauchtung*

Ihr ergebener Freund

Yours ever

Augustin Rubio

Je ne jure pas *du tout* depuis assez longtemps

Je suis assez bien Dieu merci

Love to May.

I remember when I played the Adagio from the Elgar Concerto in Westminster Abbey we all climbed up to the organ loft. Rubio insisted on coming too and sat next to Margaret. The organist was, I must say, a little heavy-handed and Rubio struck the arm of his chair with such vigour that it made the poor organist jump, then turning round to Margaret said in a loud voice, 'He play terrible, comme un pied!'

Dear old Rubio, he was so true to his art and such a friend. The last time I saw him he was walking along the Fulham Road and seeing a faded flower in the gutter, he picked it up and put it in his buttonhole.

One day when I was studying with Rubio in our London flat, the telephone rang and I answered. I could not believe my ears! I was asked to play the Elgar Concerto with Sir Edward at the Queen's Hall. What an honour and what a thrill.

Before the concert I went to London to choose my frock. It was heavenly turquoise blue chiffon and it fitted perfectly and suited the cello so well.

Beatrice also wore blue underwear on this occasion, and thenceforth according to her sister Margaret, in the superstitious way of artists, she always considered that it brought her luck if she wore blue knickers when playing the Elgar!

The great day arrived and dear Sir Henry Wood gave up practically the whole rehearsal to the Elgar Concerto which went better than I expected. Then came the concert. I think Sir Edward was very anxious.

I kept thinking of Lady Elgar who had just passed away. I thought so much of her kind words when we recorded at Hayes and I felt strongly that she was near the cello helping to make the work appreciated. Sir Edward conducted wonderfully and the orchestra was magnificent; in fact the beloved Concerto received a tremendous ovation, and since has become one of the most loved cello works.

The next day Beatrice received one of Elgar's characteristic and charming notes from Severn House:

I must send you one word of sincere thanks for your exquisite playing yesterday. I hope to have the pleasure of hearing you play the concerto many times.

With very best regards

Believe me to be yours sincerely and gratefully,

Edward Elgar

That summer Sir Edward came to see us. He wanted a dog and after a solemn investigation of our family of Scotties, he chose an adorable female. Sir Edward was thrilled with her and called her Juno (thereafter referred to as 'the goddess') and she lived to a ripe old age. Dogs were the consolation of Sir Edward's later years, his constant companions. As well as music this was another bond between us as at the time we had some sixteen Scotties, several other dogs and Margaret's menagerie of tortoises, fish and birds.

During this visit Sir Edward told me he had arranged for me to play the Concerto at the Three Choirs Festival at Hereford.

The concert was a triumph. The Manchester Guardian *critic said of Sir Edward that he conducted with 'a precision and ravishment of feeling that left no particle of the music outside his emotional influence'. Beatrice too received much warm praise but that which she valued most was from the composer himself.*

9th September 1921, Brockhampton Court, Hereford . . .

It is not right you should thank me – I thank you most sincerely for your exquisite performance of the Cello Concerto. Everyone was more than delighted . . .

With kindest regards and again thanks

Believe me to be Yours sncly

Edward Elgar

How excited I was. It was such a happy time and dear Willie Reed,* who knew the work so well, was such a great help to me.

After this I brought out the Concerto in Vienna, where it was enthusiastically received. The orchestra was very sympathetic and gave of their best. For the second part of this concert I was joined by my sister May and we played the Double Brahms which brought back memories of our tours in Europe before the 1914 war.

When I returned Elgar had been asked to give a concert of his works at Manchester and he had chosen the Cello Concerto and I was to have the joy of playing it with him. It was at this concert that before I went on the platform, Sir Edward turned to me and said, 'Give it 'em Beatrice, give it 'em. Don't mind about the notes or anything. Give 'em the spirit.' And I hope and think I did for the Press was magnificent.

---

* William Reed (1876–1942), a close friend of Elgar whom he advised technically in the composition of the Violin Concerto, took part in the first performances of the composer's Violin Sonata, String Quartet and Piano Quintet. He was leader of the LSO, 1912–35 and taught at the RCM.

7

Foyle Riding and the Nightingales

Soon after this we had to leave the farmhouse as the people who let it wanted it back. We had to look for another house and we decided that it should be in the country. My sister Margaret had passed her driving test, so she drove Mother and me in our little car on a tour of investigation. We passed many villages until we came to Oxted, which was then very tiny, and beyond Oxted was Limpsfield, one of the most heavenly corners of Surrey. We stopped at a cottage which was for sale. It was intensely cold weather but we got out and knocked and a charming man came and greeted us. I remember that there was a well outside and that it was a small cottage with three bedrooms, a drawing-room and a little kitchen. It was not at all the sort of house we had in mind for our large family but the sun was setting behind the hills beyond and, looking at Mother, I saw she had that faraway look in her eyes. I knew it so well and, as I expected, she said, 'This will be our home.'

So we came to Foyle Riding and began the great work of making our home and garden. It all progressed rapidly. A small room which Mother called her sanctuary was added to the cottage and a dressing-room for Father. Our lovely sixteenth-century table, one of our greatest treasures, fitted in perfectly. The water was laid on and the garden began to take shape. We had six gardeners and by the summer the garden began to look gorgeous. The dear old head gardener had the bandiest legs I have ever seen and used the most appalling language I have ever heard but he had gentle blue eyes and was a great artist and got on famously with Mother, who put her heart and soul into that garden. Queen Alexandra sent from Sandringham a quantity of seeds of all the blue flowers, and we had blues of every shade. In the front garden which was a riot of colour, we had roses of every variety, including the Gloire de Dijon rose beloved of Delius.

The following spring was glorious. How we enjoyed living in the country! The wood was filled with bluebells and primroses and all the lovely flowers of springtime. As the nights began to feel warmer I had a sudden longing to go out into the woods surrounding the garden and play my cello and gaze on the beauty of it all as the moon peeped out through the trees. I sat on an old seat which surrounded an ivy-clad tree. I began to play, very lazily, all the melodies I loved best and to improvise on them. I began the *Chant hindou* by Rimsky-Korsakov and after playing for some time I stopped. Suddenly a glorious note echoed the notes of the cello. I then trilled up and down the instrument, up to the top and down again: the voice of the bird followed me in thirds! I had never heard such a bird's song before – to me it seemed a miracle. The sound did not appear to come from the high treetops but from nearer the ground; I could not see, I just played on and on.

The next day I got up early. I was thrilled. I ran straight to our old gardener and asked him what that glorious bird could have been. He nearly fell over with joy and delight. 'Why it's that night-ingale come back once more, after so long. Were you playing to him, Miss?' He had heard the cello in the wood. I nodded my head. 'Why, then you have brought him back to these parts – don't ye let him go again.' I said I would try to keep him and every night I wandered through the wood playing and listening to the heavenly bird, my only audience being the rabbits and once a tiny shrew which came and sat on my foot. Alas, the month of June came and the nightingale left us for a whole year, but the cello never forgot the voice of the nightingale.

Work at Foyle Riding had continued all the while. An adorable cottage was built at the edge of the woods for friends, or anyone in need of a rest, to stay in. The house had been enlarged skilfully so that the atmosphere of the old Elizabethan cottage was retained. The red brick flooring and deep fireplace of the old kitchen were complemented by the addition of oak panelling which transformed the room into a delightful sitting-room. Furnished with our old Persian rugs, oak furniture, grandfather clocks and deep blue Bristol glass the house looked welcoming and warm. Margaret showed a great interest in and talent for architectural design. She drew up the plans to convert the old barn into a Music Room, and this was magnificently successful. Margaret selected the oak to panel this room completely, and high at one end was a musicians' gallery while at the other there was a public gallery which would hold a score or so of people. There was a huge fireplace; an open hearth along one side and the carvings and the richly coloured glass in the windows all gave warmth to this large room.

The gardens too seemed to have established themselves magnificently. It was quite impossible to believe that only a year before cows and hay could be found in the Music Room and a field where now roses, delphiniums and sweet williams bloomed.

We learned of the romantic history of the Manor of La Foyle, of which the cottage of Foyle Riding was part. As early as the thirteenth century it had been let for the yearly rent of a clove of gillyflower, so of course we made sure that plenty of these old-world flowers still breathed their scent across the beautiful flagstones of the garden.

The Harrisons could not wait to share all this beauty with their friends so they decided to have a party, the first of many at Foyle Riding. They sent invitations to see their new home, their gardens and their Music Room together with 'a very little music'. They invited not only their London friends and their friends in the musical world but also many of the villagers of Oxted as they hoped that their Music Room would become a focal point for local music and drama. They wanted to put on concerts for the village people to attend.

Princess Victoria, together with Lady Fitzwilliam, her Lady-in-Waiting, came down. Tea was served on the lawn overlooking beds of lupins and the goldfish and lily ponds. Amongst the other guests noted in the Evening Standard *of 21st July 1923 were Lady Worthington Evans and her daughter Lady Blanche Beresford, Mr and Mrs York Bowen, Roger Quilter, Arnold Bax, Cyril Scott, the sculptor Sir Alfred Toft, Sir James Denham, Edwin Evans and Mr and Mrs Eugene Goossens.*

After tea I played the *Chant hindou* and a little Kreisler piece in the Music Room, the audience being made up not only of our guests but also of our sixteen dogs and the Princess's adorable pekinese Punchinello!

That autumn I played the Elgar Concerto with Sir Edward at the Three Choirs Festival at Gloucester. The Concerto received a great ovation from the many musicians there.

I played many times with Elgar and how I loved these concerts! I remember his great joy was to go out with my sister Margaret for a long motor drive before a concert. She was by now a first-rate driver and Elgar always tried to make her drive as fast as possible. 'Quicker, quicker!' he used to say until they were travelling at seventy miles per hour. My sister said he laughed like a boy and although I doubt whether Margaret laughed quite as much, they both came back after a race refreshed and ready for the concert.

When Margaret was unable to drive us the remarkable character Charles Tyrell did. He had a taxi and would drive us back from our studio in Sloane Square to Foyle Riding. He kept his taxi magnificently polished and soon became one of our great friends and would telephone us daily for orders.

He helped us over the matter of Gerry. One day I had a telephone call from an animal hospital saying that they had a tiny
donkey, only a few months old, whose mother had died. It belonged
to a very ill ex-serviceman who desperately wanted it to have a
country home. We were in London because I had a big rehearsal
day, so having got hold of Tyrell and having found the address, off
we went. It took many lumps of sugar to persuade the donkey to
enter the taxi with Mother and the cello but eventually, with many
grunts and sighs, he got in and we drove off merrily. He had a very
affable look until we drew to a halt at a bus stop when, to the
amazement of the passengers, he put his head out of the window
and gave a loud bray. The sight of a taxi with a baby donkey and
a cello was too much for them, they laughed and laughed. At last
Gerry arrived at Foyle Riding and was left in the garden looking
strangely forlorn. Although he had a lovely shed my sister May
feared he might be cold and so she gave him an old but still beautiful coat, a Paquin model, and it was a wonderful picture to see
Gerry trotting round the garden with a Paquin creation tied round
his middle.

Spring was coming, and what a spring! Once more my heart
turned to the beauty of the garden. Would the beloved nightingale
come back? All the blossoms from the seeds we had planted in the
blue garden were full of colour. It was like heaven!

All those years ago it was so truly country; now sadly it has
changed so much. Our wood went straight from the garden through
a little gate where the bluebells were bluer and every tree, every
shrub seemed more brilliant. At night, the moon gave the wood a
fairy look and as I sat on the old seat surrounding the oak tree,
where I had sat before and began to play, the heavenly voice
responded once more.

After doing this for several evenings I suddenly stopped and
thought, 'Why should I be the only being to have the joy of hearing
the nightingale and the cello sing together? If only it were possible

for people, even at the other end of the world, to hear him, those who have never heard the most exquisite bird sing.'

The next day I played the Elgar in London with Sir Edward himself conducting and it was broadcast. The recording of sound and above all the broadcasting of it so that millions of people can enjoy it, has impressed me very deeply as one of the miracles of the modern age. Rex Palmer was the announcer on this occasion and I told him of the nightingale and my great wish. He was most interested and thought that it might be arranged. After a few days I telephoned Sir John Reith at the BBC, who seemed very dubious at first. Meanwhile the song of the nightingale was at its height at Foyle Riding and I knew that it must be now or never as from now on he would sing later and later at night and in two weeks he would be gone. I must confess I had a hard tussle, as the BBC would not believe that such a thing was possible and thought that it would be a waste of their time, a wild goose chase to come down to Surrey! But I knew that the good God wished the world to hear the duet of the cello and the nightingale. For nights I had crawled to find whence the most thrilling notes might ring out.

At last however it was agreed and Captain Eckersley, Captain West and other engineers came down with Mr Rex Palmer who was to announce. It was something to see all the paraphernalia of the BBC in our garden. It was a great risk of course, as in those days no wild bird had been broadcast before in its natural state. It was a thing so new that they all, engineers included, seemed to think it impossible. Of course in those days it was 'Cat's Whiskers' and '2LO calling'.

A sensitive microphone had been set up within a hundred yards of where the nightingale sang so that the notes could be picked up, amplified with a suitable amplifier and then transmitted by land lines to '2LO'.

At about nine o'clock I crept up with my cello to a ditch and placed my chair half in and half out of it, quite crooked, but I knew that the exquisite voice was there, under a thicket of oak leaves, ready to sing to his little wife. I played for what seemed hours, praying all the time.

Curious noises did take place, heard through the microphones: rabbits biting at the wires, strange little sounds from insects and squirrels and then – oh dear – Gerry the donkey, now a year old, had in some way got out of the shed in which he had been shut and was braying loudly. He saw one of the engineers crawling towards the nightingale's nest with a microphone and skipped up to him, gave him a push, upsetting the microphone, and galloped off in high glee! The poor man had to pick himself up and begin again but still the nightingale did not sing.

Suddenly, at about quarter to eleven on the night of 19th May 1924, the nightingale burst into song as I continued to play. His voice seemed to come from the Heavens. I think he liked the *Chant hindou* best for he blended with it so perfectly. I shall never forget his voice that night, or his trills, nor the way he followed the cello so blissfully. It was a miracle to have caught his song and to know that it was going, with the cello, to the ends of the earth. My excitement was intense. My greatest wish was accomplished!

Evidently the whole world had been waiting and from the letters I received, that quarter of an hour had given the greatest pleasure. I gather it was heard by about a million people and that the music of the Savoy Orchestra stopped abruptly as the song of the nightingale was relayed. It was heard in Italy and in Paris and in London. Many people who did not possess receiving sets listened to the bird's song by telephone from friends who had loudspeakers!

The broadcasting experiment was repeated, even more successfully, the following week and arrangements were made to install two microphones the following year. The public, I must say, went completely mad over the nightingale, the experiment touched a chord in their love of music, nature and loveliness. I received thousands and thousands of letters; one old gentleman from New Zealand said that he had left the old country when he was a boy and to hear the song of the nightingale once again, out on a New Zealand Farm, was a prayer answered. Many of the letters were just addressed to 'The Lady of the Nightingales, England' or 'The Garden of the Nightingales, England'.

How I thanked my mother and my whole dear family who had believed in my idea and helped me, they were all wonderful. So was the BBC and so was the nightingale. But I had one old friend who, I am afraid, did not appreciate the more mundane results of my propensity for playing in the open air. That was the gardener. 'I loves your music, Miss,' he said to me, 'but I do wish it didn't attract them birds the way it do. They eats up all the fruit, something cruel.'

Many people came that summer, every hour of the day and night, and however hard I was working I had to welcome them and show them the garden, for they were all so interested and enthusiastic.

It was a busy time and that autumn Sir Edward Elgar honoured me by asking me to play the Cello Concerto with him in Worcester Cathedral. I was the first woman instrumentalist to play there, and I believe that Sir Edward had some difficulty in persuading some of the dignitaries that all would be well, as some of them seemed uncertain. I tried to dress very suitably in a lovely frock of red and gold velvet with a long train and a head-dress of gold net surrounded by pearls and round my neck I wore Mother's cross of emeralds and pearls. The atmosphere of the cathedral was like no other and something greatly spiritual descended on the cello and I know the orchestra experienced it too. The following year I played at Gloucester Cathedral and the next at Hereford and always the same feeling of serenity was with me.

After a tour of the British Isles I came home. Spring was with us again, once more the nightingales came back and the hush of the woods and garden was more fairylike than ever. The BBC came down again; also HMV came and made some enchanting records of the nightingales and the cello and of the other birds at dawn. They were a phenomenal success, many thousands being sold. Hundreds of people came every day and at night as well. Alas, we could not refresh them all. They all seemed to love the garden and the atmosphere of the woods. They came from Canada, India, China, Japan, Australia, New Zealand and America. One of the most delightful of our visitors was Mr Ford and his wife. His one wish was to buy Foyle Riding and live there and he did not quite understand that what one loves best one would not sell for any amount of money, but he was always courteous and seemed to enjoy himself.

We also chartered buses from Stepney and the East End of London to bring hundreds of little children with their fathers and mothers under the wing of their parson and they all had a heavenly evening up to midnight. We hired large trestles, cups and saucers, and two huge teapots, one on each side of the trestle, and every kind of dainty to tempt them. Mother and my sisters poured out while Father and I served them, and the men were given tankards of beer. They enjoyed the thrill of the bluebells, which some of the little ones had never seen, and the wood where the nightingale sang. One dear mother of ten children told us that the nightingale seemed to sing for them alone, and so it was. At midnight they climbed into the buses with the parson and set off for home. I do not think these people ever forgot those nights spent in our beloved garden and woods, with the moon shining through the trees and the cello and the nightingale. Many more people came the next year and the next year, always with the same enthusiasm.

During all this time I was, of course, playing at many interesting concerts. It was my joy to bring out the works of living composers and I brought out the Cello Sonata by Arnold Bax with Harriet Cohen at the Wigmore Hall. Bax did me the honour of dedicating this sonata to me and he remained a friend of the family and especially of my sister May, until his death. I also gave the first performance of John Ireland's glorious Cello Sonata with Evlyn Howard-Jones. A little later that year I introduced this work at the Salzburg Festival, once more with Harriet Cohen. I also brought out the Irish Melodies, arranged in an enchanting setting by Herbert Hughes.*

I met Zoltán Kodály at one of the Three Choirs Festivals. I think it was at Hereford the first time. One of his works was being performed but I remember that poor Kodály looked terribly bored. I had received a copy of his Sonata for Solo Cello from a great friend, Edwin Evans. He was most enthusiastic about it and told me to go and hear it brought out in London. When I heard it I thought both the Sonata and the player very dull.** However, I began to work at it and, my goodness gracious, how difficult it was at first to get used to the strange tonality, putting the C and G strings down a semi-tone, and playing in the key of B minor. Of course I had to arrange my own fingering because of my small hand and I had to work at the big stretches by putting an empty cotton reel between my thumb and first finger and work my hand in this way by the hour.

Kodály's wife Emma was adorable, her only wish always being to arrange marriages. At one of the Festivals I saw her go up to a renowned professor, a confirmed bachelor who was sitting talking

---

* Herbert Hughes (1882–1937), Irish composer and critic, co-founder of the Irish Folk Song Society, arranged a series of Irish songs, *The Kilmacrenan Edition*, for violin and cello. Several were dedicated to Beatrice who helped with the fingerings and bowings of the cello parts, and some were regularly performed by her.

**Kodály's Sonata for Unaccompanied Cello had been given its first performance at Salzburg in 1923. Beatrice played this work twice in 1924; in February at a Contemporary Music Centre concert in London, and then on 8th May at the Aeolian Hall. This latter concert was billed as the 'first public performance in England' and the *Morning Post* critic referred to the performance as 'its first in London', so it would seem that Beatrice must here have attended a private performance.

to a middle-aged lady, and ask them, with an engaging smile, 'Are you two going to be married, yes?' The poor man jumped and the poor lady turned bright red – they had never met before! Emma just trotted off to find another couple; she was so romantic.

When they came to visit us some years later, Kodály wished to hear the Sonata once again but he would not listen to it in a room, insisting on my playing it in the garden. As the weather was rather damp, my peg disappeared into the grass! Still I played it for three hours, Kodály giving me a wonderful lesson, and at the end he said, 'That's all you can expect with a hand that size!' Nevertheless he did seem satisfied.

At that time the Kodálys were very poor but also very proud. With a gentle smile Emma refused all financial help, accepting only our friendship.

Cyril Scott wrote a fantastic and wonderful piece for my cello and orchestra called *Philomel*, which I played with Beecham. Scott also wrote a piece for cello called *Pastoral and Reel* which imitates the bagpipes most perfectly and is thrilling to play.

I became acquainted with Lawrence Brown, the accompanist of Roland Hayes, the famous negro tenor. He was a delightful person and most enthusiastic. He used to come down to Foyle Riding and fry chicken for us, just as it was done in the Southern States. It was after this, in the Music Room, that he taught me to play the beautiful negro songs and I was able to catch their unusual rhythms which pleased him greatly. He arranged these songs for me and we gave a concert at the Wigmore Hall which attracted so much attention that it was completely sold out.

The Daily Telegraph *music critic said:*

Mr Brown has given these beautiful tunes an unobtrusive background calculated to set off their natural charms to the best possible advantage and Miss Harrison's . . . employment of a slow portamento could readily be accepted as a successful attempt to produce one of the most characteristic features of negro singing.

About this time Elgar honoured me greatly by asking me to play the Concerto on the night when he was presented with the Royal Philharmonic Gold Medal [19th November 1925]. I then made further records of it with him. I remember he was very gay and told me it did not really matter what happened to the orchestra as all faults could be put on the soloist. How we laughed (at least I did not laugh as much as he did!). However, he seemed very pleased with the records. I think and hope they were a great success.

Between all these concerts I was playing once more in the gardens and woods. Crowds and crowds used to come − geographical societies, gardening societies, ramblers and many others. Oh, how tired I used to get! I am afraid that once I was caught looking at a whole family from Birmingham who arrived at lunch-time. I was wearing what was known as my 'electric smile', which at times I switched on and off. I did not want to let them in but they gazed so long at the gate that in the end I went to greet them. They were most enthusiastic and charming and at once I felt sorry. This visit seemed to stick in my mind because afterwards my mother gave me the text of that wonderful saying 'I shall pass this way but once'. I have it still and often look at it and think.

Mother had an extraordinary understanding of those who needed consolation. I remember a friend, quite a young man, who had been through Gallipoli and although not physically wounded, the memory of that campaign would not go from him. Mother had him and his wife down and they had the beautiful cottage to themselves and mother would talk to him by the hour trying to bring back his faith in life. He got quite well and never forgot.

13 Supervising the building
   of the Music Room

14 Playing in the Music
   Room

15 The party to celebrate the opening of the Music Room. Princess Victoria with Beatrice

16 'a sudden longing to go out into the woods surrounding the garden and play my cello . . .'

17 & 18 'All the paraphernalia of the BBC': wireless engineers
fix the microphones for a nightingale broadcast and take
up station outside the front door of Foyle Riding

19 Beatrice makes a record with the nightingales for HMV

20 Beatrice at Foyle Riding, 1925

21 Tea at the Malvern Festival, *circa* 1935. *Far side left to right:*
Margaret, George Berhard Shaw, Beatrice, Mrs Shaw,
Miss Gwendolen Lally and Sir Barry Jackson

22 'My small hands'

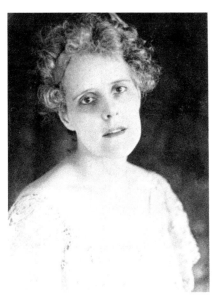

23 Beatrice after her
mother's death in 1934

24 Beatrice and
Margaret performing
in the early 1950s

25 Beatrice in the early 1960s with Frank Salisbury's portrait 'Pietro and Beatrice'

8

Fêtes Champêtres and
Sixpenny Concerts

The following winter I went to Paris to introduce the Kodály. It was while I played with the Lamoureux Orchestra that I saw him again, that strange young man who had haunted my tours in Europe before the war. Now older-looking of course, but still the same thin face, the same intense gaze. Now, surely we would meet. But no, he slipped away at the end of the concert as he had so often done before.

I did not have time to dwell on this matter for my next concert was at the Salle des Agriculteurs with Joseph Salmon who had harmonised some old cello works in the most exquisite way. He accompanied me himself in these works by Tartini and Dupuis. I also played the Kodály and some new Herbert Hughes, accompanied by Margaret. All were most enthusiastically received, for which I was most thankful as Paris audiences are notoriously difficult for foreign artists.

A couple of months later Joseph Salmon and I put on a similar programme at the Wigmore Hall. Also around this time I played the Haydn Concerto in D under Malcolm Sargent at one of the Robert Mayer Children's Concerts, an experience I enjoyed and which I repeated several times. It was a very busy time.

In the month of March 1926 alone, Beatrice played at the Wigmore Hall, the Aeolian Hall, the Queen's Hall, the Albert Hall, the Central Hall and the Palladium; she then went to Holland and Vienna.

It was approaching the time when I was to go to America to bring out the Delius Concerto and Sonata and the Kodály. Before this however, I went to visit Delius with Mother, Margaret and Gerald Moore. Delius was very anxious to hear his Sonata and Concerto before I took them to America. He also wished to hear Margaret play one of his Violin Sonatas, as he was so fond of her. We arrived at Paris and proceeded to Grez. At the small station we mounted a small bus. The whole of one side was occupied by a man with a pointed beard and very sharp teeth. Under the seat were four guns and there were three large Alsatian dogs with him on the seat. Our party, with the cello, violin and luggage, had to squeeze into the opposite seat, where he regarded us with a sinister look.

Was this an omen? I don't know. However, it was too late to go to the Deliuses' that night and dear Jelka had booked us into a pension nearby. In so doing she must have mentioned my name as 'Baba' and the proprietors had not unnaturally concluded that there was a baby in the party and instead of a bed, had provided a cot! Further, there was no bedroom at all for poor Gerald, who had to sit up all night in the coffee room. The next day, rather tired and very hungry, we went up to the Deliuses' for lunch. Jelka put a chicken leg on Gerald's plate, saying with great decision, 'That is for you, Gerald.' Then she gave Margaret and me the wings and Mother a very little breast, as most of it had to go to Fred. I think it must have been a very old chicken because when Gerald tried to cut it, it was so tough that it flew to the other end of the room. He heaved a sigh, but did not try to retrieve it. The wings were quite impossible to eat and seeing everyone in difficulties, Mother could not help going into gales of laughter.

After this lunch, I played to Delius and although he was so ill he seemed happy and enthusiastic and we talked much of America and the forthcoming tour in which I was to bring out his works.

In spite of the domestic mishaps, this visit is one of my most treasured memories.

It was a great honour for me to bring out the Delius Concerto in America but unfortunately, although other items in my programme were very successful, the Concerto was not. The Philadelphia Orchestra was very good to me but alas, Stokowski, their conductor who loved Delius's work, was away. Fritz Reiner conducted for me and he could not bear nor understand Delius's music. If I had played Dvořák with him all would have been well, as he loved it. Neither Delius nor I had any idea that he would be conducting; it was such a shame. Delius had so longed for his Concerto to be brought out. I must confess that the people did not understand the idiom of Delius and although I hope it did not sound difficult, so many passages written for the cello would have sounded perfect on the woodwind. If neither Press nor conductor grasped it, the orchestra loved the work and when the Philadelphia Orchestra came over to London many years later with Ormandy, it was a great pleasure to find that many members, including the first violin and oboe, remembered the Delius with delight.

At the same concert I brought out the Kodály – and it was a great success! The conductor in New York was Mengelberg and he did not like the Delius either. As he shook hands with me after the concert he said, 'Ah, dear me, that was beautiful, but could not Delius have given the work one scratch?' He did so miss a big climax and the Delius is of course utter serenity. With a smile I remembered the garden and the peace when he sketched it out.

The beautiful arrangement by Herbert Hughes was very well received, but in America I think no success of the old cello has ever touched that of the Kodály Sonata for Solo Cello. The public was mesmerised by its strange moods, the passion and the peace and the strange technical effects of the work. It put the cello on a level with other instruments; in fact even more wonderful than a fiddle, as I do not think any other stringed instrument could put the lower strings down a semitone and play in the key of B Minor instead of C Major.

The Delius Sonata, with Margaret playing the piano part, was sympathetically received.

We were staying with our dear friends the Thayers. One of my happiest recollections is of the delightful hours Mother and I spent with Mrs Roosevelt Senior. She was a wonderful hostess and often took us to see the President and his wife. I used to listen, highly entertained, as he and Mother had long and wonderful talks together. When Margaret and I returned to Washington later, he invited us to see him, and talked so much of my mother.

At last it was time to leave Philadelphia as this was not a long tour; I had gone over only to introduce the new works. Our English friend, Miss Hillier, who was extremely patriotic, was ill and she insisted on giving us her parrot, feeling that if anything happened to her, England would be the only place for Waw-waw, as he was called. Before leaving America we stayed a few days in New York and a kind friend lent us a really gorgeous apartment in Park Avenue. Mother set off on grand shopping expeditions, for frocks and hats for the girls and women she loved to help. For many summers afterwards, we would see Oxted ladies tripping about in frocks and hats from America, of styles never seen in England and of all colours; and the hats, what dreams!

At last all was packed and off we set from New York. Waw-waw seemed very excited. We had a rough journey which made Waw-waw roll about singing hymns and shouting, 'It's a long way to Tipperary' with enormous expression and vibrato. When we arrived at Southampton it was midnight but the authorities thought fit to disembark us. We were worried about importing the parrot as there was a Bill going through Parliament because of parrot disease. The officials were very sleepy and cross but many had heard the

nightingale broadcasts, which was a help to us. At last they came
to Waw-waw. 'What have you here?' asked the official. After a few
minutes of utter silence a voice came from under the black cover,
''ello me darling!' said Waw-waw with a giggle. 'Let them through,'
was all the official said.

This reminds me of a later time, when Waw-waw was established
at home. A very nervous individual came to see us and we pressed
him to stay to tea. As he sat with his back to Waw-waw, clutching
his tea-cup, a voice, soft and low, suddenly murmured, ''ello me
darling.' The poor man jumped. He thought it was one of us!
Waw-waw tittered in an amused way and I could almost see him
winking.

Once back from America, I made a short visit to Italy, a country
I find quite wonderful, although on this occasion I only visited
Rome. I played in the Accademia di Santa Cecilia to a very large
audience amongst whom Mussolini was reputed to be present. I
played the Kodály and also brought out a Sonata in three movements by Manilo di Veroli, a young Italian composer, a native of
Rome. The following day I went to the Vatican and played to the
Pope, which was a great honour. During this visit I was presented
with a glorious Processional Cross which seemed to me a symbol
of serenity and peace ever after. Mother was very anxious to meet
Madame Garibaldi, who was very charming to us and we had a
delightful time and returned home happy and refreshed.

That summer we gave a wonderful pageant in aid of the British
Legion at Foyle Riding. We had fourteen acres of grounds, and
tents were erected and every sort of amusement was offered.

*Some of the items from the programme of the Grand Gala and
Musical Fête:*
*Bands of The Royal Engineers, The London Irish Rifles Drums
and Pipes Band, The British Legion Band*

The Russian Balalaika Orchestra
Chester's Marvellous Performing Dogs
Lotto — The Famous Trick Cyclist
The Famous Calno Trio — Gymnasts, Trapeze, Equilibrium etc.
Professor de Hempsey Conjuring, Punch and Judy
The Checks Concert Party
Reg. Wishart — the Mystifying, Merry Magician
Styo — the Great Hoop Juggler
Les Treborres — *Novelty Entertainers*

Gerry the donkey had an enjoyable time being a perfect nuisance amongst the tents but this fête was the occasion of our meeting a most extraordinary individual, the Marquis d'Oisy. He was sent by a big London store to see if there was any artistic work he could do. He was also an exquisite designer of frocks. He made one for me the colour of an iris with hand-painted irises along the train. I have always thought that he was a Cockney but he called himself a French Marquis; no matter, he was a great character and helped to make the pageant a huge success. I remember he belonged to one of the groups of folk-dancers, he was at least six foot four and danced most beautifully. We were all dressed as shepherds and shepherdesses and we danced in the woods while he played a little pipe.

Our friends the Thayers came over from Philadelphia and stayed in the cottage near the wood. Mrs Thayer loved our midnight parties but Mr, like my Father, could not tackle them. They would stand together at the window and look down on us like two schoolboys. The next day they would say, 'And how did you enjoy your ghar-rs-t-ly night?' with a twinkle in their eyes.

The organiser of the pageant was another remarkable man, Wilfred Stephenson. He organised concerts all over England and although I have played pretty well all over the British Isles, the Continent and America, the concerts Wilfred Stephenson put on were those I loved playing at more than any others. They were for the people, for the working man, for the miners. The tickets were sixpence and he engaged the finest artistes. Margaret played the violin for him just as I played the cello. To come on to a platform, however tired one felt, and to see the faces of those dear people all aglow with thrill and sympathetic understanding was a great moment in my life. One concert I recollect was at Burnley on one of the nights when Burnley had won a football match. It was a terrible night, having snowed hard and become very slippery. We had a whole mile to walk to the Hall, as of course all the taxis had gone to the match. I grasped the suitcase and violin and Margaret took the cello and the music. Suddenly it seemed as though the whole of Burnley appeared, skidding down the road full tilt. I was terrified that the cello might be mistaken for a football by this exuberant crowd but no, they cheered us on our way with good-humoured jokes. We were rather late arriving; no matter though, there they were, if not exactly the same faces, a public full of enthusiasm and open delight.

The nightingale broadcasts and the records had brought me close to many people. At nearly every station, as I got out with the cello, porters would come up to the carriage saying, 'Is that old Peter? – let me carry him for you', or 'Have you got the nightingale with you, Miss?' The cello, I am happy to say, became one of the most famous and loved beings in the country.

I went to Berlin in the spring of 1927 to bring out the Elgar there. Alas, it was a dead failure, much to my horror and Elgar's disappointment. Werner Wolf was the conductor and he did not understand it in the least and the orchestra was as heavy as lead. I have never been back there since.

From Press reviews of this performance of the Cello Concerto with the Berlin Philharmonic, as sampled in literally translated excerpts preserved by the Harrison family, it would appear that the degree of the work's 'failure' in Germany is here somewhat exaggerated. In these excerpts Beatrice's playing is highly praised, but there is certainly evidence of some dislike of the work itself, which was clearly not to German taste of the time. 'Every note of the composer is sunny spring, full of flowers', one critic is quoted as saying, and he places Elgar in 'the melodious-romantic period after Liszt', in the company of Humperdinck and the early Weingartner. This critic's musical affiliations are clear: 'Of course, far, far away from any "atonal" revolution, the work has a true homeliness, which begins to get on one's nerves.'

One of the greatest moments of my life occurred when I was making some records at Hayes for HMV. I had stopped playing for a few minutes when suddenly the door opened and King George V walked in. I knew he was making a private tour of the building but had no idea he would come into the room where I was playing. He came straight up to me and before I could even curtsey, said, with such a charming smile: 'You have done something I have not been able to do. You have drawn the Empire closer together through the song of the nightingale and your cello.' Then, after chatting for a few minutes, he left. I shall never forget the emotion it gave me, or the kindness of the King's smile.

Soon after I went to Holland. It was a joy to be there again. I love the Dutch audiences, they are so sincere! I shall never forget the experience we had at Rotterdam. Margaret accompanied me and I was to bring out the Delius Sonata and the Kodály Sonata. I had been told before that, in this city, an audience never clapped until the end of a concert to make sure that they liked one's playing, but I could not quite believe this until it happened, and it did! The hall was full but as I came onto the platform with my sister there was dead silence. I bowed, I played the first Sonata – not a murmur. All we could hear was our own footsteps going off the platform. It happened again and again until the end of the concert when a storm of applause broke forth and I was so very, very thankful!

I made a tour right through Holland on this occasion and I met Gustav Holst, who said he hoped to write something for the cello, but alas, he died not long afterwards.

Then I was off to America again. We sailed on the *Homeric* which I believe was the first liner to run on oil. Mother and I were given the State Suite (I have never quite known why) on the top deck. There were wonderful beds, a lovely sofa for the cello, and a grand bathroom. When we arrived the customs officer asked if the cello were 'Old Peter', his friends in England having written with enthusiasm about the nightingale broadcasts after a visit to Foyle Riding! How I loved the cello being known to the ordinary public.

On arrival I was to broadcast in the Atwater Kent hour. I had asked if, after I had played, I could talk to the people about our English garden and how I came to bring back the nightingale to our district through the cello. I was very anxious to invite Americans to come and visit our English home and hear the cello, the nightingales and the wild birds.

Dear old Sam Franko conducted for me, and then I had to speak. I think I must have rehearsed my few words for two hours! Mother, being the sister of Charles Charrington, the great theatrical producer, made me speak every phrase as though it were music, with crescendos and diminuendos, as she said articulation was very important as my voice had to carry to every State of America, as well as to England! Mr Atwater Kent was there himself. I think he was as thrilled as I was.

London Passing Show

Wireless Enthusiast—I wish that beastly bird would shut up—they're broadcasting a nightingale singing in a few minutes.

FRIEND: "What is your husband doing up there?"
HOSTESS: "Just trying to recall the nightingales to sing to us again."
DRAWN BY G. S. SHERWOOD.

News of the nightingale broadcasts spread far and wide. *Top*: cartoon which
appeared in the American newspaper *Public Ledger*, 20th May 1929.
Above: cartoon by G.S. Sherwood in *The Sketch*, 9th July 1930

Under the gracious patronage of H.R.H. *the* Princess Victoria

SATURDAY MAY 13 at 4 p.m.

in aid of the Royal Society for the Protection of Wild Birds

A NIGHTINGALE FESTIVAL

Organised by **BEATRICE HARRISON** with the kind
assistance of the Gramophone Co. (His Master's Voice)

in the famous grounds of

FOYLE RIDING · OXTED · SURREY

**The gardens and woods will be open till dawn on Sunday
refreshments at low rates available during the whole time**

Admission **1s.** Children half-price

BUSES WILL MEET ALL TRAINS AT OXTED STN.

Poster for the Nightingale Festival held at Foyle Riding in May
1933

*Beatrice concluded her talk on Sunday 27th January 1929 with the
words 'I shall be delighted to have any one of you who is planning to
visit England next spring or summer, come and see my fifteenth-century
cottage and the old world gardens and hear the nightingales in their own
loved surroundings.' She then gave the full address twice and spelled it
out!*

I played at ten p.m. in New York, which was three a.m., five hours later, in England. At Foyle Riding my beloved family sat up to listen and I was told, thank God, that my voice came through perfectly. Father's only remark, as I invited all those American people to come and be welcomed by me, night or day, was, 'My Godfathers, she does not know what she has done!' and then he went to bed, as he said, 'to await events'. I shall never forget the delight of playing with Gabrilowitsch and Sapelnikoff and their kindness to the cello.

I had a successful tour extending from New Orleans to Colorado Springs, where I played in the little church where Charles Kingsley preached in years gone by – I seemed to feel his presence still there.

In Virginia I went to visit a wonderful park where some small alligators were kept. The head keeper pressed me to choose any alligator to take home to England. I assured him that I had never thought of such a thing but he seemed truly disappointed. He offered me one which he said was an old lady of a hundred and twenty years of age. She was three feet long but somehow I felt I could not lead her round the deck on the way home. I also thought of the shock to my poor father if greeted by a three-foot alligator. After much consultation with my mother, who I knew had Margaret in mind, we decided on two small alligators, Jefferson and Virginia. The head keeper was absolutely delighted about it and had them packed in crates and sent on to New York to await us.

Then it was time to return home, together with the alligators. I decided not to cable Margaret as I wished she should have a surprise. And so they were! Father looked thoughtful and rather sad. Of course Margaret was thrilled. The problem was where to put them. They had to be kept warm so we put them in a tin bath on four bricks in an alcove in the dining-room. There they remained, winking an eye at us and eating raw meat until poor

Virginia died and I wondered (and secretly hoped) that Jefferson would follow her to Kingdom Come from grief. Not a bit, he grew fatter and fatter. However, we found out that he would not live on raw meat alone, but wished for live mice. None of us had thought of this and it came as a great shock. The old boy looked at us with a glassy (and hungry) eye and I had an awful, dark feeling that we ought to buy mice for him but Father absolutely forbade it, *alors voilà!* Help came in an unexpected way. The telephone rang and it was a man with a charming voice asking if he could come over and see the garden with his wife. We welcomed him but he did not fall in love with the garden as much as with Jefferson. He was a great motor racer and told us about his pet monkey. Suddenly a thought came to me. Margaret had always longed for a monkey. Why not exchange the monkey for the alligator? This was arranged and Jefferson left us and James the monkey began his reign at Foyle Riding.

Spring came – and again the BBC broadcast the nightingale's song. Once, when the nightingale was in a rather damp and dank part of the wood, I came across a circle of frogs all croaking and looking at the cello with great interest. The croaks came through in the broadcast, but no matter, it caused more interest.

About two thousand Americans came that summer. One morning the English Speaking Union telephoned to say that a party of ladies from an American gardening society were making a tour of English gardens and wanted to see the Garden of the Nightingales. My mother said we should be delighted to receive them but forgot to ask the exact time they would be arriving. Thinking it would be the afternoon she tripped forth to London with my sisters to purchase wine and food for refreshments. I was left to work and Father, a great mathematician, was at home working on a problem. Looking out of the window he saw a fleet of cars, at least thirty of them, coming up the road. He came into my room with a serious look to tell me of the arrival. We both looked out of the window and then at each other. The next moment I was alone, and I saw Father, in his old panama hat, welcoming them. The ladies trooped into the garden and it gave me a sudden shock to see that each carried a small notebook. I felt stunned when they asked for the names of each and every plant and shrub. The terrible thing was that I did not know the names and yet I could not disappoint these ladies from every corner of the States. Taylor, our dear old gardener, had the morning off, so there was no help from that quarter. The only thing was to make up the names of plants and shrubs I did not know and this I did with as much feeling as possible, getting rather wild about the spelling. By the end of the visit they all looked happy and when Mother came home she laughed until the tears ran down her face.

I then went to France to visit Delius. I was to introduce his *Serenade*, a cello arrangement of his incidental music to Flecker's play *Hassan*, also some cello pieces he had written for me, to American audiences on my next tour which was forthcoming.

Before this however, I had a sudden engagement in Dublin, to take the place of Madame Suggia* who was ill with an attack of influenza. It was a big concert given by the Roman Catholic Church. Mother had many friends in Dublin and was delighted to come with me.

I was just beginning the concert when I glanced at the balcony where Mother was surrounded by priests. I played Handel's *Largo* but imagine my surprise when I rose to bow and saw the whole row in the balcony empty. When I came back to take a second

---

* Guilhermina Suggia (1888–1950), the enormously popular Portuguese cellist, studied with Julius Klengel in Leipzig and lived with Casals from 1906 to 1912, settling thereafter in England, where her striking appearance became known to many through Augustus John's portrait. In many ways she was Beatrice's closest rival, but the rivalry was friendly as both women were blessed with extremely good natures and their fields of interest were somewhat different.

bow, there they all were again, helpless with laughter. It appears Mother had dropped her purse and the whole row had gone on their hands and knees picking up pennies!

Then home again to our lovely woods and garden. Watching wild birds had always been a joy to me and so when I heard that Lord Buckmaster was preparing a Bill in parliament to prevent skylarks being sold in East End markets and blinding them to make them sing, I felt impelled to help. We decided to hold a Nightingale Festival to collect signatures for the Bill. We prepared refreshments and opened the grounds of Foyle Riding from four p.m. until dawn.

The weather for this Arcadian event was warm and fair and the correspondent of Bird Notes and News *said:*

> A gay company streamed about the gardens and woods throughout the afternoon and evening. The nightingales happily did not disappoint listeners, for when they sank into silence and possibly disapproved of the lights of a mile of motor cars that flowed over the car park, the chink of plates and the many voices, Miss Harrison wandered down the glades with her magic instrument and lured them to song once again.

Mr Oliver Pike gave a lecture illustrated with his own films and we obtained a thousand signatures for the Caged Birds Bill. The contributions which the public made were donated to the Royal Society for the Protection of Birds and we felt happy that an unusual evening for which people has come from all over the British Isles had benefited birds in every way.

It was wonderfully quiet and peaceful time at home which was always a great joy for me. My younger sisters were presented at Court, Margaret having my exquisite frock of Malines lace by

Reville Terry. My sister Monica, who was tiny but extremely gay, with a lovely voice, also had a heavenly frock with a long train, and she held a small bouquet of roses. My Mother wore her exquisitely beautiful wedding dress, which she later gave to me and which I have worn at many concerts. It was powder-blue and silver and the collar of lace was worn by my great-aunt at the famous ball given on the eve of the Battle of Waterloo. Mother looked magnificent but the night before Father had been taken ill and her worry was so great than when she was dressed in all her court finery she turned to Margaret and said, 'I feel just like a Queen from Honolulu'. I have never known why!

How thrilled my sisters were. My small sister balanced her train perfectly and was so delighted and overjoyed at seeing the King that she waved her bouquet at him and he was mightily amused and told our beloved Princess all about it.

Almost every Sunday afternoon Margaret and I used to go over to play with our Princess at Coppins, go over to play with our Princess at Coppins, her home near Iver. We were always welcomed by her adorable Pekinese Punchie, who came to know the sound of our car's horn and always rushed out to have a word with us before we went in. Then, when we had told all our news, we used to play by the hour. Of all the music, it was the slow movement of the Elgar Cello Concerto the Princess loved best. I wanted to give her something that would always remind her of it, so I asked Mr Hal Broun Morrison, a great-nephew of Holman Hunt and a genius at damascene work, to help me. He made a glorious little book of damascene – the front had a model of the cello with a nightingale singing on top. At the four corners were placed moonstones and at the bottom was an uncut ruby (which is a symbol of great love). On the back of the book was a falling star and it was bound by Mr McMillan with an A string belonging to the cello. The pages were vellum, and my sister Margaret copied, most exquisitely, the cello part of the slow movement of the Elgar. The pages being so small she could only copy two bars on each page. Sir Edward Elgar signed it and the book was a complete joy to our 'Blessed Damozel' as we called the Princess. It never left her and when she died it was her express wish that it should be sent back to me.

9

'The setting sun, and music at the close'

Then came the greatest tragedy of our lives. My mother, the inspiration of my music and all things beautiful, passed away. It was her voice that taught me to sing on the cello – our music together was something out of this world and I often dream of it now. I remember our Rector used to call her the 'Socialist Conservative' and he loved coming up to Foyle Riding for the people's parties she gave. Hundreds of people from all walks of life, mothers with children, village shopkeepers, musicians would have tea in our Music Room with our beloved Princess pouring out tea for them with us. My Mother gave herself to others and the world seemed desolate and bare without her.

The grief and shock almost killed poor Father who was already ill at the time and he died soon afterwards.

Delius died the same year, and his wish was gratified and he was buried at Limpsfield, quite near my dear parents. On the day of the re-interment in the month of May, the flowers had never been more glorious, just as on the last day he had been at Foyle Riding. On that day Beecham came with a portion of his orchestra and played amongst other works *On hearing the first cuckoo in spring*, as only he can conduct it. As the work finished, a cuckoo from a nearby bough took up the refrain, which gave an eerie feeling. Poor Jelka Delius, who was really dying, came over for the ceremony but was too ill to attend. She passed away a few days afterwards and is buried next to Delius, in that peaceful and beautiful churchyard of Limpsfield.

For us, thank God, there was so much work to do that there was little time to show one's grief. In spring Margaret came with me to Italy on tour. On our arrival from England, feeling tired and homesick, as we passed the barrier in Milan, the ticket collector suddenly burst into an Italian aria. He was singing it to the cello which was being hoisted on to a porter's shoulders while a queue of people gathered. It was a lovely moment and I was quite charmed and so was the cello.

I brought out the Delius Concerto in Milan, Rome, Venice and Bologna and it had a very great success. I also brought out other English works and they all pleased the Press and the public immensely. Rome was glorious – the whole city radiated with flowers and exquisite perfumes and we stayed there and wandered about. It was a lovely rest.

After this I returned to America with Margaret and what a glorious tour we had. I played the Richard Strauss Sonata in F with Henri Deering and in Philadelphia I played in the Sanctuary of the Graphic Sketch Club, one of the most extraordinary places imaginable. The Sketch Club had been founded for the purposes of bringing art to all with no distinction of class or creed and the Sanctuary at its hub is like a highly decorated church stuffed with art treasures of all the religions of the world. The motto is 'Enter this Sanctuary for rest, meditation and prayer. May the beauty within speak of past and ever continuing ways of God' and is addressed to 'the patrons of the busy streets of Philadelphia'.

We played at a very large luncheon party given by Mrs Eleanor Roosevelt. The dining table was decorated with carnations, snap-dragons and ferns and was incredibly pretty. I played some of my favourites, Roger Quilter's *Amour de Moy*, *Blackbird Reel* by Herbert Hughes and *Serenade* by Delius. The guests included many ambassadors and ministers from overseas with their wives. Margaret and I enjoyed ourselves a great deal.

Quite a contrast was provided when we played in one small town in Texas – the audience seemed to consist mainly of cowboys, thrilled to see a cello and even more to hear a woman play such a large instrument. Margie and I put on our best frocks and as encores played some of their own songs, which I had learnt, as I did so want them to love the cello. They were on their ten toes with joy and, after the concert, they escorted us back to our little hotel, calling us to come back again, which alas we never could.

We wended our way back to New York and there I played at one of the most brilliant 'At Homes' of the season. It was a party given for Prince Valdemar of Denmark. Everything in America seems so much bigger and so much more luscious than anywhere else. The blaze of colours and the extravagance of lights was immense. The hostess was a perfect darling, very sweet and very stout. Her whole frock seemed to consist of diamonds and on her head was a tall erection of precious stones that twinkled every time she moved. After the music we climbed on two chairs just to get a better look at the people. The Prince was enchanted with the beloved cello and we had a gay and lovely time.

How sweet the American people have been to me and how I love them. Unused to my instrument and intrigued with it, at first how they wondered why I, a woman, ever played it! How well I remember in Memphis once, a man stopped me in the street the morning after a concert to tell me how much he had enjoyed the music. He had never seen a cello before.

The time had come to return to England. I was sad to leave kind Mrs Thayer who had looked after us so lovingly; she had lost her husband and seemed glad to have Margaret and me and the cello.

That summer in England, Sir Barry Jackson* asked me to go down to the Malvern Festival to play the Elgar Concerto with Adrian Boult. I think those Festivals were one of the greatest joys of my career; the next year I played the Dvořák Concerto and the year after, the Haydn. Sir Barry Jackson was a perfect host and made one feel at one's ease at once. I met many famous people there, amongst them Bernard Shaw, who was so kind and gentle to me. I shall never forget the expression in his eyes after the slow movement of the Elgar! He sat in the front row with such an intense gaze; how he loved music, it seemed he was in another world. He and I often talked about music.

Here is a letter which GBS wrote to Beatrice at about this time.

Ayot St Lawrence
21st November 1936

My dear Beatrice Harrison,
    We are too old to go out at night in this weather. Charlotte is quite desolate, Handel and YOU being her special musical loves. But what can you expect at eighty?
    I shall reproach the BBC for not broadcasting the recital. It will do them good to be told that you are the greatest cellist in Europe, and therefore presumably in the world. That confounded nightingale probably got you listed as Variety. They know no better, blast them!
    always yours
    G. Bernard Shaw

---

* Sir Barry Jackson (1879–1961), who created the influential Birmingham Rep in 1913, founded the Malvern Festival which flourished for nine years, bringing together the best of British music and drama, including Elgar and George Bernard Shaw, who was a friend of Jackson.

The death of my beloved Princess Victoria occurred soon after-wards, and oh how I missed her and her wonderful friendship and advice, in so many ways, and how often did I long for her. What a void it was and how lonely for the cello. My world seemed empty, so many loved ones gone and, with Mother, gone too the thousands of people she had helped. In my great solitude I turned to my beloved cello trying, as always, to reach the Heavens, and my mother's presence seemed strangely near.

Just before the last War, Margaret, Monica and I left Oxted. May had already lived in London for some time. We felt terribly sad and downcast but at last we found an adorable old house [Woolborough Farm at Outwood, Surrey]. It had been the Palace of the Bishop of Southwark in the twelfth century and it had a yew tree one thousand years old. The house was small and most of our beautiful furniture had to be packed into the barn. One could still see how the pilgrims had trodden down the stone floors of the house and I believe it had been a hiding place for Charles II. It had a fairy-tale atmosphere, but those days were sad for us and it was difficult to smile. Then even sadder, the War came. It was declared on Monica's birthday. After Mr Chamberlain had announced it, a record I had made of the *Caprice* of Delius was played and, ever after when I played this piece, it reminded me of that fateful moment.

We had many enemy planes and doodlebugs over our heads and at times it was strange looking out of our small windows to see a German airman baling out during the Battle of Britain. We were frequently under bomb attack and the British guns were placed so near that pieces of shrapnel nearly hit us as we passed from room to room.

My life was very full, trying, with my music, to give peace to those so much in need of it. I thought at first to join ENSA but nearly every musician had joined, so I wrote to a friend, Christopher Stone, who I knew could help me by giving me the names of hospitals that most needed music. Margaret and I also gave concerts all over the country for the troops, and I think what I loved best was to hire a small van, put our tiny piano into it, the cello, the violin, Margaret and myself, and drive to different gun outposts and give them a little music to cheer them up. Sometimes after driving for miles we would be caught in a raid and have to stop. I used to cover the cello with my body and the little van I used to hide if possible. Then on we went. We always had the same driver, always cheerful and such a help.

It was at this time that our beloved Uncle Charles, Father's brother, who had done so much to alleviate the pain and trouble of others, came to our little house to spend the autumn of his life. Before this he had lived in South Kensington where he would go out sometimes all day, trying to rescue bombed people, until finally he was bombed out and had to leave London. He was in his ninetieth year, and his serenity was such a comfort to us in those dark, dark days.

Travelling at night was the most terrifying to me. There was always the danger, in the blackout, of getting out of a train on the wrong side of the line with the cello in the pitch dark. At concerts however, how wonderful the British audiences were during a raid. I have had the experience of a doodlebug hovering over the concert hall, making one wonder what the next moment would bring. Even when the red light went up under the platform and the guns were going, not a soul moved. There were funny moments too; on one occasion I had just started the *Serenade* by Delius when there was a noise like thunder and eight hundred armoured cars dashed past! The only thing was to shut one's eyes until they passed. I shall never forget how the kind audience smiled when I began again – such a comfort to me.

We had some delightful gunners posted near our house, and what a great thrill it was to cook their Christmas dinner for them. They had a large piece of pork and an immense turkey and they were extremely agitated as they had no oven or anything big enough to cook these delicacies in. We volunteered of course, but oh dear, the size of our oven was minute. However, with a great deal of manipulation, the pork was got in and the oven door shut bang and eventually a lovely smell issued forth. The turkey was a greater effort because of the breastbone, but at last by four o'clock all was ready and the men sat in a circle with a big old mastiff bitch, Bess, which we had given to them, in the middle wearing a tin helmet!

During the very bad raids I received a contract to play in a film produced by Anthony Asquith. It was a propaganda film* to complement and contrast with the one called *Mrs Miniver* which showed the effects of war with people living in shelters. In this film all was to go on as usual – even the nightingale was to sing. I believe that the Minister for Propaganda himself was playing some records during a terrible raid, amongst them the cello and the nightingale. It struck him suddenly, why not have this record in the film if possible, as it sounded so fantastic against the banging of the guns? The scene was to be a beautiful garden and I was to play near a lake, with the nightingale record playing, hidden at a distance.

Margaret, the cello and I set off, during a raid as usual. Filming was fascinating to me. The story was of a Russian who came to see how we lived during the bombardment. I had to say a few words and as I arrived at the studio a kind engineer asked if he might carry the cello for me and I answered, as I usually do, 'No, thank you, I always carry him myself.' These few words seemed just right. In the film I was announced by the butler to my rich host, played by Felix Aylmer, and that was my cue to say these words.

---

* *The Demi-Paradise* (1943), starring Laurence Olivier as the Russian who finds nothing quite as he expects it in England.

The film was sent out to the East for the troops to see and a friend who was stationed in Burma saw it and said that when he saw me sitting by the lake playing, he nearly went mad with joy as it was all so truly English. It was shown several times and he sat through every performance.

One of the most delightful memories of this awful time was when the Italian prisoners came to work round the farm. Their great joy was music and they much preferred listening to the cello to getting on with their work. One day I was playing 'Amarilli, mia bella' when a glorious tenor voice joined in and sang with the cello. There was much clapping and jollity and I had to go down and show them the 'glorious Pietro' as they called the cello. After that they came every morning and we had lovely music.

At about this time dear Uncle passed away. He was buried with full military honours as Father had been before him. Many, many people came to his funeral. Just after this we had the most terrible raid. About midnight a terrifying crash came upon us. I always had the cello next to my bed and I felt out in the dark to see if he were safe. My sister was lying stretched out on a sofa under the beautiful processional cross I had been given in Rome. There was always a feeling of great serenity about this cross, some feeling about its loveliness that is not of this world, and being in its shadow I felt sure my sister was safe. The doodlebug had in fact been shot down within a few yards of the house but we were all safe. The barn in which our treasures were stored had gone, the doodlebug had crashed right into it. The only one who enjoyed it was the parrot Waw-waw who sang throughout. The soldiers came to see if we were all right and we were, although very shaken.

After such a tremendous shock it was wonderful to go out into the beautiful orchards. Gerry, our little donkey, came up to us. All outside was as always, only the barn and the wrecked doodlebug spoiled the beauty of nature.

All through, concerts took place. People craved for music and the Proms kept going, thanks to the great soul of Henry Wood. He was the kindest friend of the people and of artistes. My sisters and I loved him; his great ideal was to help young composers and musicians and it was indeed sad when he died. He was a friend of the cello from the very first concert I gave at the age of twelve when, in the middle of the Saint-Saëns Concerto, which I was playing with such élan, the pike (an old-fashioned one) suddenly ran down and, with beating heart and crimson face, I had to stop.* With great sympathy and kindness Sir Henry got down from his rostrum and helped me to fix it, and then we had to begin all over again. How happy, therefore, I was to play in the Proms during the war.

One of my great joys at this time was sitting to the portrait-painter Frank Salisbury. I was painted with my cello and the picture was called 'Pietro and Beatrice'. This took place during the fiercest raids, but Mr Salisbury made me forget the terror of bombs.

When the hateful war was at last finished we realised that we should have to look for a new home. Margaret had formed a partnership with a great friend of hers, May Atfield, and they founded the famous kennel of Sanctuary Irish Wolfhounds, my sister's favourite breed.

At last we found an ideal spot to house ourselves, our instruments, our dogs, birds, fish, cats (seven saved from the war), our donkey and all our furniture. What a move it was! A kind farmer lent us a float (there were no furniture vans to be had). On this we placed two grand pianos, our donkey and the farmer's son. Margaret made twenty journeys a day for several days in 'the old Liz', our car, elderly but still doing a brave job. I felt sad at leaving our old farmhouse, the yew tree, the pond with the ducks and

---

* By strange coincidence the début of Jacqueline du Pré in 1961 at the Wigmore Hall was marred by a similar incident; her A string gradually slackened until she was forced to stop.

the sanctuary it had offered us during the terrible days of the Battle of Britain. I think as one grows older some things become more vivid, such as the beauty and goodness of people, and the terrors fade away.

The house we took [at Nutfield Ridge, Surrey] is built on high ground, having a most glorious view of fields of every shade of colour. It is very large and although the rooms are lofty and big it could never, for me, have the atmosphere of the little farm.

As we moved in it had a desolate air, with no electric light and we were only able to find one candle! And how cold it was. The night after we arrived there was a grand ball in the village. For some strange reason I had clung to the hamper in which the best concert frocks had been packed, and so by the light of the candle we arranged ourselves and went off. Everyone was most jolly and the evening became distinctly rowdy.

The next thing was to put in the electric light, but who to do it? At last we got hold of a most strange being, half-Egyptian and half-Irish. He had just married his seventh wife (quite true, although it sounds like fiction!) and he arrived with several of his sons. He said he would have to stay for three weeks, so we put them in the top of the house and daily they pulled up more and more floorboards. This man had a most enchanting son of about fifteen. He was a child of the sixth wife and he used to keep us in fits of laughter telling us about all his mothers as evidently they were all great friends. I was rather nervous of the man himself as he used to cast amorous glances at me and the cello. Sometimes I would ask the boy to shut the door of my practice room and not to let his father in. He used to grin and say, 'I don't blame yer Miss, Dad is already thinking of his eight' wife!'

Work and concerts went on for me and the dog-breeding flourished. Our friend John Gielgud telephoned at this time and asked if five of the Irish Wolfhounds could appear in the hunting scene of the opera *The Trojans* at Covent Garden. Margaret accompanied them and had a great time behind the scenes and this began a tradition of our dogs appearing at Covent Garden which went on for years.

May would come and spend the week-ends with us and many of our friends came to see us in our new home, and so I was not very surprised when the telephone rang one day and a voice asked me, in French, if he might come down and visit me, this being his first visit to England. I said I would be delighted but imagine my utter surprise when a little man arrived whom although so many years had elapsed, I recognised at once as the individual I had first seen in Warsaw and later at Leipzig and Paris. The thin-faced young man was now older of course, his dark hair grey but unmistakably him. He told me he was a Russian, a cellist, himself at one time a pupil of Becker. He had been thrilled at hearing the cello, so much so that he had followed my career but had never dared go round to the artistes' room. He told me that he had been once more to Warsaw and had been to see the first cellist, then an old man. He asked if he remembered my cello and the old man brought out the very programme of that Warsaw concert from his pocket book where he had kept it all those years, and on it were written the twenty encores I had played that evening after my solo with the orchestra!

My visitor told me that he was also a writer and that he wanted to put a chapter about me in a book he was preparing in France. He told me that my memories were of interest and that is how I came to begin to write them down.

As I think of my years of work and of the great joy my audiences have given me, I realise that my beloved instrument has been my life and my staff. As long as I had the cello with me, even during the war when bombs could have smashed us both to pieces, I had no fear and felt a peace.

Now, as I look out of this window, through the wrought-iron gates towards the woods, it is a joy to gaze beyond and dream once again of the bluebell woods of long ago and the cities and the music and all the wonderful memories and above all of my intense love of the cello which has been the meaning and purpose of my life.

> 'The setting sun, and music at the close,
> As the last taste of sweets, is sweetest last,
> Writ in remembrance more than things long past.'

Afterword

When this book was first published in 1985 the name Beatrice Harrison, whilst known to musicians and music lovers, was not one with which the general public was very familiar.

Since then, and I think the autobiography played a role, various events have occurred to bring this remarkable woman to a wider public. They show that now, a hundred years after the iconic broadcast of her cello and nightingale duet, Beatrice Harrison is by no means forgotten.

Beatrice Harrison was far more than a great cellist, she was an innovator. Having heard the nightingale in her garden respond to her playing, she wanted to share this magical experience with the masses of people who did not have the benefit of a country garden frequented by songbirds. This was particularly relevant at the period when the nation was still coping with the losses and sadness of the First World War.

In 1924 she saw the way to do this was to make use of the new technique of radio which was used by the fledgling British Broadcasting Company to broadcast her playing classical music such as the Elgar Cello concerto. Her idea was ahead of the time and she needed great determination to get the BBC to come to her garden to make it happen, the first time wild bird song had been broadcast – but she did.

In 1989 Beatrice's sister Margaret, herself a gifted violinist who had lived in retirement for many years, turned once again to the world of music and with David Candlin formed the Harrison Sisters' Trust, a charitable trust to 'promote study and research into the works and lives of late nineteenth and early twentieth century British composers'. The Trust owns musical scores, correspondence from famous musicians and composers, pictures, photographs etc. and has proved a valuable resource for scholars and writers.

Also in 1989 The Harrison Sisters' Players was launched following a concert at Limpsfield Church to celebrate Margaret Harrison's ninetieth birthday. Since then the Players have given over 120 concerts in which talented artists both young and old, many from the Royal College of Music, have performed, often focusing on music from the Harrison Sisters' repertoire.

Soon after publication I gave several interviews including one on *Woman's Hour*, and I later wrote a radio play of *The Cello & the Nightingale* based on the 1924 broadcast. This play, in which Diana Quick played Beatrice and Julian Lloyd Webber played the cello, was first broadcast in 1992 with several repeats including one in 2021.

In 2004 I wrote a stage play also called *The Cello & the Nightingale* about the four Harrison sisters which was put on at the Theatre Royal, York, with the late Brigit Forsyth, herself a very gifted cellist, playing Beatrice.

Over the years several BBC regions and other TV companies have tried to recreate the 1924 event by sending a cellist into the woods hoping that a nightingale will respond. As nightingale populations have dwindled and they no longer sing in the woods at Foyle Riding, Beatrice's Surrey home, bird sanctuaries with resident nightingale populations have often been chosen for these experiments.

This was the case in 2006 when I joined the American music-ologist David Rothenberg who was making a BBC 4 documentary, *Why Birds Sing*, featuring cellist Andrea Hess, who succeeded in coaxing a response from a nightingale in a bird sanctuary in Kent.

In 2012 I took part in an episode of *The One Show*, a BBC TV programme presented by John Sergeant during which cellist Clare Deniz also managed to duet with a nightingale.

Beatrice was the first to recognise that the concept of birdsong responding to an instrument (or vice versa) was something unique, and it is particularly gratifying to see how many sound artists have run with this idea and produced works, some avant-garde, which bring Beatrice's idea well into the twentieth century.

In 2012 Yannis Kyriakides wrote a cello solo, *Beatrice and the Nightingale*, in which an extract of a nightingale's song is slowed down by a factor of sixteen and brought into the range of the cello. This transcription is woven together with a fragment from one of Bach's cello suites Beatrice Harrison had recorded, the *Prelude from Suite no 6 in D major*, this is time-stretched to bring it into the time-frame of the nightingale song, and just hinted at rather than stated through the use of silent fingerings or quiet pizzicato. The piece is a duet for solo cello as a meditation on the question of how we imagine that birds might perceive human music.

In 2014 writer and folk musician Sam Lee, who writes in his book *The Nightingale* that Beatrice 'changed his life', compiled a BBC Radio 4 documentary, *Singing with the Nightingales*, to mark the ninetieth anniversary of the original broadcast. In this film Sam sings and we also hear a recording of Beatrice herself talking about that evening in 1924. Sam now hosts a series of nightingale events in Sussex woods.

Cathy Haynes, the Chisenhale Gallery's artist-in-residence in London's Victoria Park, conducted an experimental project, *Stereochron Island*, which re-imagined Victoria Park as a fictional state campaigning to liberate itself from mechanical clock time. For the final study in 2014 she presented an innovative piece, *Dusk falls on Stereochron*, which, as she puts it, 'is a reboot of Beatrice Harrison's radio performance'. In the work, Natalie Rozario, a prize-winning cellist who studied at the RCM, responds via her cello to the natural sounds of the darkening evening when time is effectively told through shadows and birdsong. Although inspired by Beatrice, in this performance instead of the birds singing to a human tune, Rozario's challenge was to perform to theirs.

Also in 2014, award-winning audio-visual artist Kathy Hinde produced her first art installation inspired by Beatrice Harrison when she was invited to create a work for the TÖNE Festival at Fort Amherst in the Chatham Historic Docks. The artwork helped raise awareness to protect a threatened woodland nearby where nightingales sang.

This installation, *Twittering Machines*, explores environmental concerns by focusing on the nightingale, one of the only birds to serenade by night with its beautiful yet mournful song. It also ponders on humankind's ongoing fascination with understanding and categorising birdsong and animal communication.

The installation consisted of a number of rooms. To set the scene and introduce the story, a repeating 78rpm vinyl record playing on an old Dansette record player featured Beatrice Harrison playing her cello and the nightingale joining in.

The second room housed a vinyl pressing of a morse code transcription of John Keats' 'Ode to a Nightingale', also playing on a Dansette record player. The blips and bleeps were listened to live by bespoke computer software which translated the Morse back into the poem and projected it on to the opposite wall. As people entered the room and made sounds, the translation was interrupted, and the poem turned to nonsense, as a metaphor for interruptions of suitable habitat leading to a drop in the population of nightingales.

On the way upstairs a film of Bavarian bird imitator Helmut Wolfertstetter gave a nod towards the rumour of Maude Gould's imitating the nightingale for the first broadcast. The upstairs room was filled with origami birds and a vinyl record played the interrupted 1944 radio broadcast of Lancaster bombers. In the final room a mechanised swannee whistle installation imitated birdsong.

The festival featured three prominent cellists, so there was always a presence of live cello playing in close proximity. Since then Kathy has continued to develop these ideas into a live audio-visual show which she continues to tour.

Kathy collaborated with artists Jony Easterby, Mark Anderson and Ulf Pedersen in 2014 to create *For the Birds*, an immersive walk from dusk into dark. In *For the Birds* a cellist plays, accompanied by a recording of the nightingales from Beatrice Harrison's garden. This art piece highlights the drop in the population of nightingales – hence having to make do with the recording.

In 2015 Sandee Brown bought The Old Barn, formerly the Music Room at Foyle Riding. There, musical events are staged with a focus on Beatrice and her repertoire. The first concert was held there in June 2016 when cellist Adrian Bradbury and the late Oliver Davies performed pieces by Delius, Quilter and Piatti.

In 2019 street artist ATM brought a meeting of Extinction Rebellion in Berkeley Square a painting of a nightingale on a Wellington bomber. This referenced the occasion in 1942 when, as the BBC began the eighteenth annual broadcast of the nightingale, the microphones picked up the sounds of 197 Wellington and Lancaster bombers en route to Germany. Realising a live broadcast of the bombers could warn Nazi spies of the impending attack, the broadcast was quickly cancelled. However the lines were still open and both nightingale and bombers were captured on acetate disc – a haunting combination and yet another example of how Beatrice had inadvertently created another iconic moment.

That the cello and nightingale duet does somehow evoke the period is also indicated by its mention in the 2021 film *The Dig*, about the excavation of Sutton Hoo. In the film the character Peggy remarks, 'There's a wonderful cellist called Beatrice Harrison. In the summer evenings she used to practise in the garden. One night she was playing a scale and a nightingale joined in. At first she couldn't believe it . . .'

Also in 2021, cellist Anjali Tanner read Beatrice's autobiography, after which she contacted me to let me know she had spoken about Beatrice to a friend in Dutch radio, as a result of which on 23 March a short programme on Beatrice was presented by Carine Lacor on NPO Radio 4 (now NPO Classic).

Elizabeth Andrews is another classically trained musician who is starting to expand her work into the world of sound art. She grew up in Surrey but was born in Sweden, and the Surrey hills together with the Swedish lake and forest where she spent her childhood summers gave her a close affinity to nature. She is now exploring this via her cello. She had known the Beatrice Harrison story for many years and discovering young fiddlehead ferns growing near a babbling brook near Leith Hill one day, she went on to create a performance simply called *Cello:nature* inspired by Beatrice, which intersperses traditional tales of nightingales and other birds and explores the sounds of nature, combining birdsong with the voice of the cello.

In October 2022 Beatrice featured in *The A–Z of Sound* session for 7–12-year-olds held at the RCM London by The School of Noise. This was set up by musician and sound expert Dan Mayfield with the aim of providing a space to explore the way sound affects our lives. The workshops, which run globally, demonstrate something about sound for each letter of the alphabet. Dan chose

Beatrice Harrison for 'H'. He told the story and a cellist from the RCM played Saint-Saens' *The Swan* whilst a field recording of a nightingale was playing through the speaker. Great fun was had by all.

Less fun was the widely disseminated suggestion in 2022 that the original duet had been 'faked' by the substitution of a hidden bird imitator for the real bird. At the time there *was* a bird imitator, a Maude Gould (also known as Madame Saberonne or Sobonoff) who appeared in the music halls. The facts about her though hardly inspire confidence: she was married to Adolphus Schroeder, a liar and bigamist; they were both arrested for spying and although she was released he was sentenced to six years' penal servitude. The claims (of which this was not the first) that she was the 'nightingale' in the first BBC broadcast were made by her descendants.

What was different this time was that on 9 April 2023, the *Guardian* newspaper ran a piece in advance of a BBC Radio 3 programme with a headline which read: 'The cello and the nightingale: 1924 duet was faked, BBC admits after years of suspicion'.

Although I had previously heard and rebutted this idea in 1992 using evidence from an old man who, as a boy, had actually been helping onsite on that evening in 1924 and seen no such woman hidden in the bushes, as the *Guardian* article continued, 'But now the BBC has acknowledged that the duet was in fact faked using a bird impressionist . . .' I realised that if the BBC were about to admit the substitution, unlikely as it seemed, we should have to accept it.

In fact this article by Dalya Alberge revealed no such acknowledgement nor did it provide any evidence from the BBC. It was surely an example of very sloppy journalism to use an eye-catching headline above a story that failed to deliver what it promised.

Further, the BBC Radio 3 programme *Private Passions*, in which it was promised more would be disclosed, was riddled with errors, the most serious being that the duet to which the panel of expert ornithologists listened in order to judge whether the birdsong issued from a nightingale or an imposter, was not in fact the one broadcast in 1924. At that date there was no such recording, as the fledgling BBC could only broadcast – the ability to record programmes was yet to come. The panel, whose opinions were anyhow divided, had in fact listened to a record made by HMV several years later.

One of the most disappointing aspects of this fiasco, however, was that in this programme, the distinguished ornithologist Professor Tim Birkhead, emeritus professor of zoology at the University of Sheffield, on hearing this recording stated unequivocally, 'It isn't a nightingale . . . it's a person.' The host, Michael Berkeley, then asked, 'Are you sure?' suggesting that this would be a shock to many people. Professor Birkhead insisted, saying he was relying on 'research by various colleagues . . . (which) demonstrated that Gould had been employed by the BBC to stand in in case the nightingale did not sing'.

Ironically, Professor Birkhead is a Fellow of the prestigious Royal Society, the motto of which is *nullius in verba* (take no one's word for it) which, in relying on these 'various colleagues', was exactly what he *didn't* do.

After hearing the recording, Michael Berkeley, who was in no way to blame, commented, 'I don't think I'll ever listen to it in quite the same way again . . .' demonstrating clearly that this had cast a shadow over Beatrice's reputation.

Although some mistakes have now been admitted and the BBC Archive has clarified the situation regarding the broadcast and the recording, no formal apology has been offered either by the *Guardian* or the producer of the Radio 3 programme.

Better things were on the way. In July 2023, Adrian Bradbury, cellist, and Andrew West, pianist, recorded a CD – *The Pre-Raphaelite Cello* – for the SOMM label, David Candlin and the Harrison Sisters' Trust having secured sponsorship.

The album features ten premiere recordings with Beatrice at the very heart of the disc. It includes Quilter's *L'Amour de Moi* which was in her programme for years. This was never published in her lifetime and was thus exclusively associated with Beatrice. Appropriately enough, the original fifteenth-century *chanson* is about a maiden in a garden with a nightingale.

Cyril Scott's *Pierrot Amoureux* is effectively a love letter in music addressed to Beatrice. As Oliver Davies wrote, 'it clearly enshrines Scott's adoration for the 19-year-old Beatrice whom he likened to a Botticelli angel and to whom he later proposed marriage.'

The idea for the CD was Oliver Davies's, so it also forms a lasting legacy to his devotion to the Harrison Sisters.

Enormous changes, both social and technical, have come about since 1924. Our world is very different now, but the magic of the cello and nightingale duet remains a moment of pure wonder thanks to the vision and tenacity of Beatrice Harrison.

Patricia Cleveland-Peck

Discography

Whilst this discography does not profess to be a complete listing of the recordings of Beatrice Harrison, it does aim to present the mainstream of her recorded legacy.

All the recordings are HMV originals. The numbers that comprise only digits are the earliest of Beatrice Harrison's recordings and indicate single-sided discs. Numbers prefixed by B and E are ten-inch double-sided discs (some of the latter coupling earlier single-sided issues). The prefixes C and D indicate twelve-inch double-sided issues.

Where Beatrice Harrison recorded a title more than once, the listing appears in chronological order.

An attempt has been made to identify correctly many of the somewhat vaguely worded titles.

Dates of recordings are not here given because in the majority of cases it has proved impossible to obtain them.

	78 rpm No.
J.S. BACH	
Gigue in C for unaccompanied cello	07897
	D 346
Sarabande	D 474
George Henschel *piano*	
Sarabandes in E flat and D (*arr.* Henschel)	2–7871
George Henschel *piano*	E 205

It has not been possible to trace copies of the above two 'Sarabande' titles which are probably the same recording.

BOROWSKI	
Adoration	C 2753
Herbert Dawson *organ*	
BRAHMS	
Cello Sonata No. 1 in E minor Op. 38	D 1380–2
Gerald Moore *piano*	
H. COATES	
Angelus	B 4399

May Harrison *piano*; Henry Coates *organ*
Based on Arcadelt's Ave Maria.

Benediction   B 4399

May Harrison *piano*; Henry Coates *organ*
Based on Mozart's Ave Verum.

CORELLI

O Sanctissima (*arr.* Kreisler)   B 3471

Margaret Harrison *violin; with piano*
An arrangement of the Adagio (4th movement) of Corelli's
Sonata in D Op. 5/1. Label states Palestrina to be the composer.

CUI

Orientale (Kaleidoscope Op. 50/9)

(i) *with orchestral accompaniment*   2–7852
                                                                 E 143
(ii) Herbert Dawson *organ*   B 3605

DAWES

Melody   B 3274

Margaret Harrison *piano*

DE LARA

The Garden of Sleep   B 4095

with orchestral accompaniment

DELIUS

Caprice and Elegy   B 3721

with chamber orchestra/Eric Fenby
Re-issued on World Records SH 224, where noted 'orchestrated by Eric Fenby'.

Cello Sonata   D 1103–4

Harold Craxton *piano*

Serenade (Hassan)   B 3274

Margaret Harrison *piano*

DVORAK

Songs my mother taught me Op. 55/4   B 2853

solo cello and nightingales

ELGAR

Cello Concerto in E minor Op. 85

(i) *abridged version* symphony orchestra/Edward   D 541 &
Elgar   D 545
(ii) *complete version* New Symphony Orchestra/   D 1507–9
Edward Elgar   D 7455–7

The session dated 24th February 1920 referred to by Beatrice Harrison in her
memoirs was postponed and the abridged version of the Cello Concerto (i) was recorded
on 22nd December 1919 and 16th November 1920. (i) reissued on Pearl Records
GEM 113; (ii) (recorded March and June 1928) reissued on EMI RLS 708 and
World Records SH 175.

DISCOGRAPHY

GRAINGER
Youthful Rapture   C 1929
orchestra/Malcolm Sargent
HANDEL
Largo (Serse)   C 1647
Margaret Harrison *piano*
Sarabande   B 3605
Herbert Dawson *organ*
This music has been identified by some as from a Concerto Grosso in G minor,
1741.
HENSCHEL
Sicilienne   2–7870
George Henschel *piano*   E 205
KRAKAUER
Paradise   C 1647
Margaret Harrison *piano*
Label details state this to be 'Viennese Melody by Kreisler'.
MACKENZIE
Benedictus   C 2753
Herbert Dawson *organ*
B. MARCELLO
Adagio (*arr.* Salmon)   B 3717
Margaret Harrison *piano*
From Marcello's Sonata in G minor Op. 1/4.
POPPER
Gavotte No. 2 in D   D 474
?George Henschel *piano*
Harlequinade   C 1626
Margaret Harrison *piano*
Vito   D 346
with piano accompaniment
RIMSKY-KORSAKOV
Chant hindou (Sadko)
(i) Margaret Harrison *piano*   E 186
(ii) *solo cello and nightingales*   B 2470
The nightingale and the rose Op. 2/2   B 4095
with orchestral accompaniment
A recording of a nightingale is also dubbed onto this studio recording.
Slumber Song (May Night)   2–7850
with orchestral accompaniment   E 143
G.B. SAMMARTINI
Grave and Vivace (*harmonised* Salmon)   B 8118
with orchestral accompaniment

Described as 'Suite ancienne' on the label, this music is the second and third movements of a Sonata in G.

SCHUBERT

Ave Maria D.839   D 345
  with piano accompaniment

Impromptu No. 3 in G   D 345
  with piano accompaniment

  It has not been possible to trace a copy of this record. The Impromptu is presumably an arrangement of the G flat Impromptu D. 899 No. 3.

SCOTT

a) **Pastorale** b) **Reel**   B 3717
  Margaret Harrison *piano*
  Only the Reel has piano accompaniment.

SELIGMANN

Chanson grecque   E 186
  Margaret Harrison *piano*

R. STRAUSS

Morgen Op. 27/4   B 3471
  Margaret Harrison *violin; with piano*

TARTINI

Adagio (*arr* Salmon)   B 2896
  with piano accompaniment
  Described as 'Sonata in C' on the label, this music is a movement from the Sonata in G Op. 2/12.

TRADITIONAL

a) **Air in B flat** b) **Blackbird Reel** (*both arr*. Hughes)   D 1195
  ?with piano accompaniment

The Bard of Armagh (*arr*. Hughes)   C 1929
  *with orchestra/*Malcolm Sargent

Lament of Fanaid Grove (*arr*. Hughes)   D 1195
  ?with piano accompaniment

Londonderry Air   B 2470
  solo cello with nightingales

VALENTINI

Tambourin (*arr*. Salmon)   B 2896
  with piano accompaniment
  The composer is described as 'Valentine' on the label. This movement is from the Sonata in B flat Op. 8/3.

VAN BIENE

The Broken Melody   C 1626
  Margaret Harrison *piano*

Index